For Lisa,
In the splendour
of sound
in St. Catharines

BARDCODE

GREGORY BETTS

With a Preface by Philip Terry

Published by Penteract Press
PenteractPress.com
Twitter.com/PenteractPress

Typeset in Minion

ISBN 978-1-913421-46-5

FIRST EDITION

Limited to 154 Copies

This is No. 75

Hello Lisa
these bright
little songs
are for you

Previous Praise for the BardCode Project

If sound is color
then syllables are light
& Shakespeare's sonnets
sing a rainbow's tune
in Gregory Betts's
stunning feats of sleight.

—Charles Bernstein, Donald T. Regan Professor
at the University of Pennsylvania

Through meticulously colour coded "rhyme groupings" of William Shakespeare's sonnets in *Sweet Forme*, Greg Betts reminds us of the arbitrary, stringent, and also nearly always invisible power relations underlying every statement, phrase, sentence, word. The result of Betts' poetical-mathematical time travel that bridges Shakespeare's time of the Bubonic plague to our current time of the Coronavirus: the transformation of well-worn poetical phrases into page upon page of gorgeous colour-sound palettes.

—Lori Emerson, Director of the Media Archeology Lab
at the University of Colorado Boulder

Gregory Betts has found 'the sonnets most true' by William Shakespeare, selecting these seven poems because they conform exactly to a grid of 140 syllables (10 × 14) without ambiguity; then he has 'paint-coded' the palette of syllables that rhyme throughout these poems, thus exposing the chromatic qualities in the musical rhythms of the Bard himself. So beautiful, so wonderful, is this exercise that I kick myself for not having thought of it first; but I am grateful to know that one of my dearest friends has done it for me, only with more pigment and with more panache.

— Christian Bök, author of *The Xenotext*

the perfect revelation of visual poetry

—Petra Schulze-Wollgast, Editor of *ToCall Magazine*

The sonic qualities and possibilities of William Shakespeare's sonnets should be obvious to anyone who has ever read them aloud. In *Sweet Forme*, however, Gregory Betts reveals to us the visual properties of the Bard's mastery of language. Creating a heatmap out of trusted stanzas, Betts makes every syllable glow and shimmer in all the hues of Shakespeare's verse.

—Joakim Norling, Editor of Timglaset Editions

Preface

Shakespeare's *Sonnets* have long been a source of inspiration for poets, who have returned to them again and again, emulating their dazzling combination of intricacy and duration, of feeling and colour, characterisation, and the dramatisation of moods. They were the initial inspiration for Ted Berrigan's *The Sonnets* (1964), and K. Silem Mohammad, in *The Sonnograms* (2009), created a whole new sonnet sequence, in rhymed pentameter, by submitting Shakespere's poems to a process of anagrammatisation. My own *Shakespeare's Sonnets* (2011) recreates the sonnet sequence from fragments of infotainment ideolects culled from the tabloid press, while in *Sleeping With The Dictionary* (2002) Harryette Mullen submits the sonnets to Oulipian procedures of N+7 to create wild refigurations of Shakespeare's forms and language. Another tradition in poetry, whose origins can perhaps be traced back to the synesthesia of Rimbaud's poem "Voyelles", where each vowel is assigned a colour – A black, E white, I red, U green, O blue – has explored colours in relation to poetry, and increasingly, since Futurism and Concrete Poetry, and developments in print technology that have made the use of colour in print cheaper and more widely available, has employed coloured inks in the *production* of poetry. Christian Bök, in one of several versions of "Voyelles", translates the poem into bands of colour corresponding to those ascribed by Rimbaud to the vowels, and the French poet Jacques Roubaud has recently turned to the use of coloured inks in his poetry to add visual currents and clues to his complex polyphonic verse patternings. And the same can be said of the sometimes digitally inspired New Concrete, as well as of visually inspired poetics more generally, as in the work of David Bellingham and André Vallias.

Armed with an interest in the New Concrete and code poetry and a full spectrum of colours, Gregory Betts's *BardCode* – his second engagement with Shakespeare following his versions of sonnet 150 in *The Others Raisd in Me* (2009) – combines these until now separate traditions, by ascribing colours to the repeated sound patternings in Shakespeare's sonnets, calibrating the frequency of each sound pattern to the level of brightness, and printing off the resultant data visualisation in (mostly)10x14 grids. The results are a series of 154 visual pieces, resembling expanded Rubic's cubes, or stained glass created by Mondrian or Paul Klee – Klee taught stained glass, book binding and mural workshops at the Bauhaus – that provide a map of the sonnets. At first glance, there's little to tell one of these visualisations from the next, but if we pay them attention they can tell us some things about Shakespeare's *Sonnets* that might otherwise be overlooked. One thing they make instantly visible is the syllabic count of the sonnets, where Shakespeare's line veers into 11 or sometimes 12 syllables, and Betts's grid expands correspondingly, creating a penumbral border to the right hand edges of the poems, foreshadowing the appearance of the "dark lady" in sonnet 127 ("In the old age black was not counted fair"). Irregularity, the breaking of rules, in a word, is made visible, and when we reach sonnet 127 itself in *BardCode*, we are confronted by a love triangle of three irregularities in the shape of three misfit lines of eleven syllables each, echoing the irregularity that Shakespeare introduces into the conventions of the sonnet sequence at this point, by introducing a new object of love who defies the sonneteer's stock range of epithets. Another thing that is highlighted in Betts's visualisations is something that we have perhaps known all along, but never articulated as clearly before, and this is that the music in Shakespeare's *Sonnets* is not confined to the end-rhymes, but is there in every syllable of every poem, demonstrating how the sounds of the poems are literally orchestrated, making liberal use of internal rhyme and repetitive sound patternings and modulations of form and colour to weave their complex music. And this in turn lets us see why rhymed poetry often fails in lesser hands, for here the music is *only* there in the rhyme, and as such is too insistent, too obvious, like a sententious drum, as in the poems of Rudyard Kipling. And this reminds us that if there is to be a future for rhymed poetry – as in the complex imbricated rhyming of Andrew Wynn Owen's *Infinite in Finite* (2023) – it needs to be in this direction. *BardCode* inaugurates a new kind of data poem, a new kind of potential literature, one which will keep researchers, academics and poets busy for some time to come, as they apply Betts's research methodologies to the poems of Spenser, Donne, Milton, Keats, Pound, Eliot, Plath and Larkin. But these poems also give us something of beauty, visual creations that, if recreated in stained glass, might grace the entrances of Shakespeare's Globe in London, and the Royal Shakespeare Theatre in Stratford-upon-Avon.

— Philip Terry

BARDCODE

GREGORY BETTS

1.

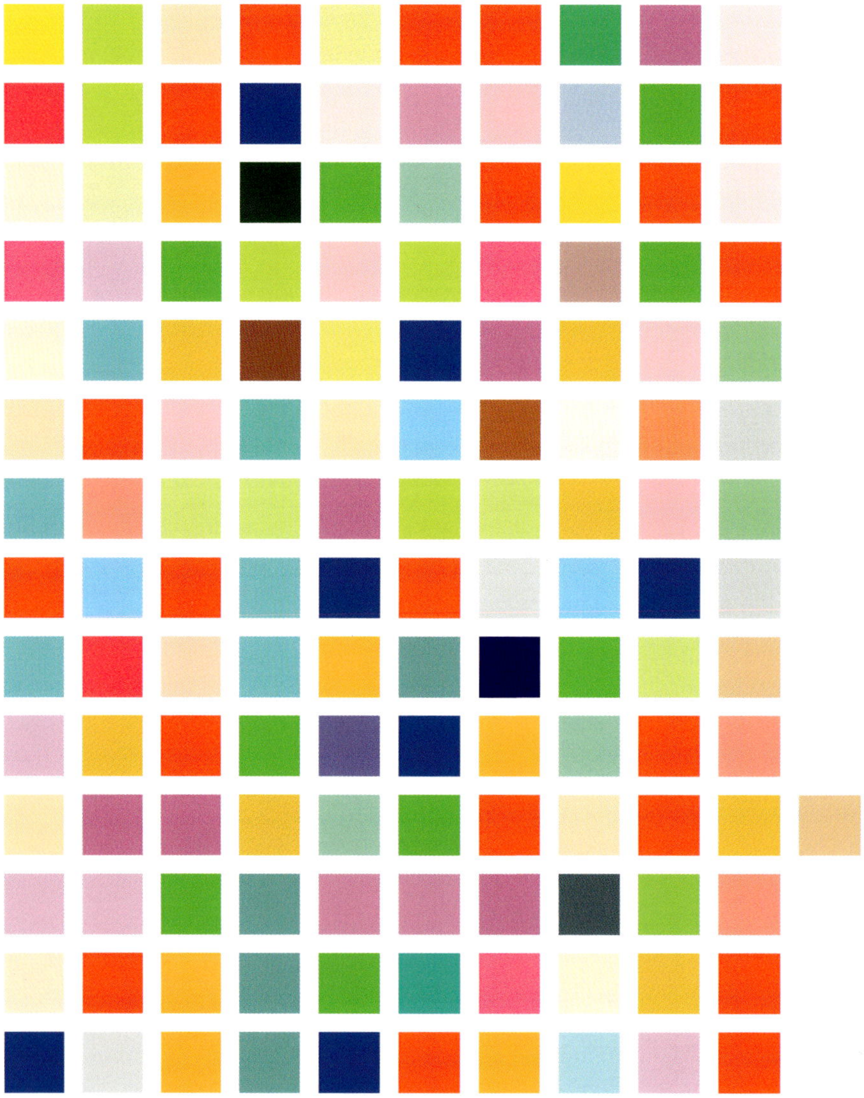

2.

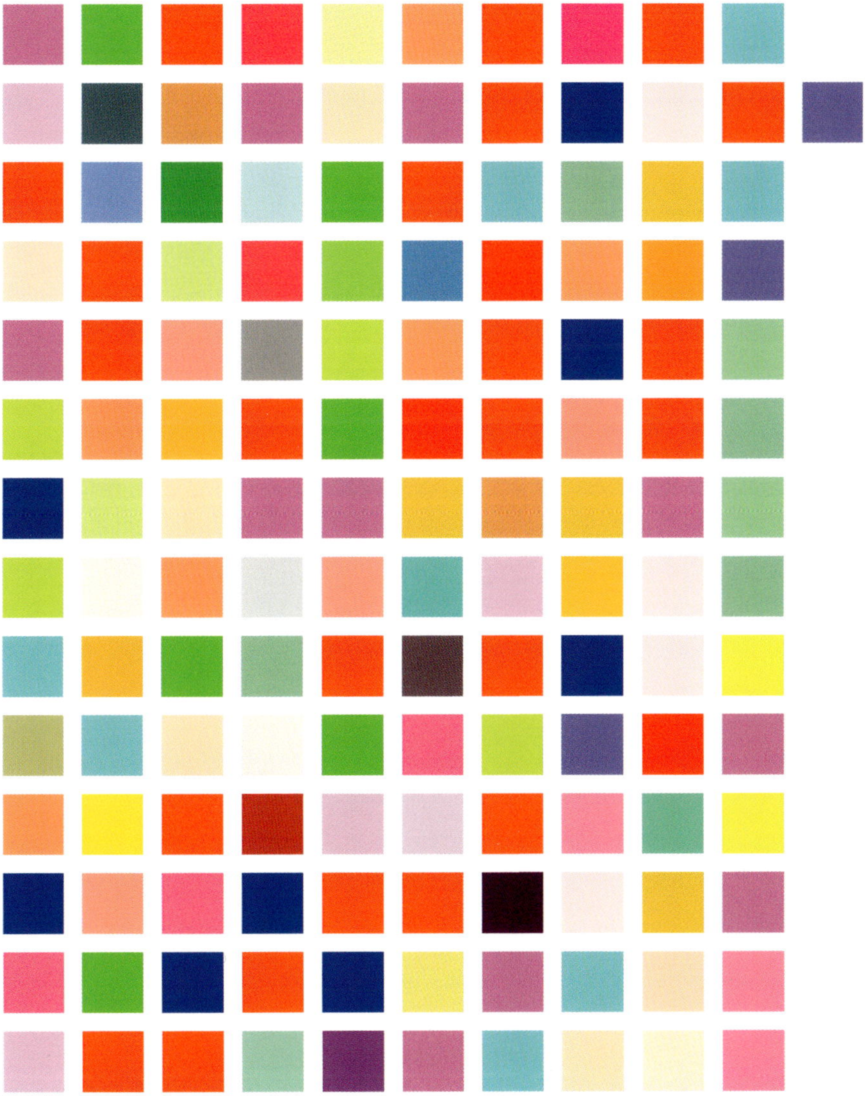

3.

4.

5.

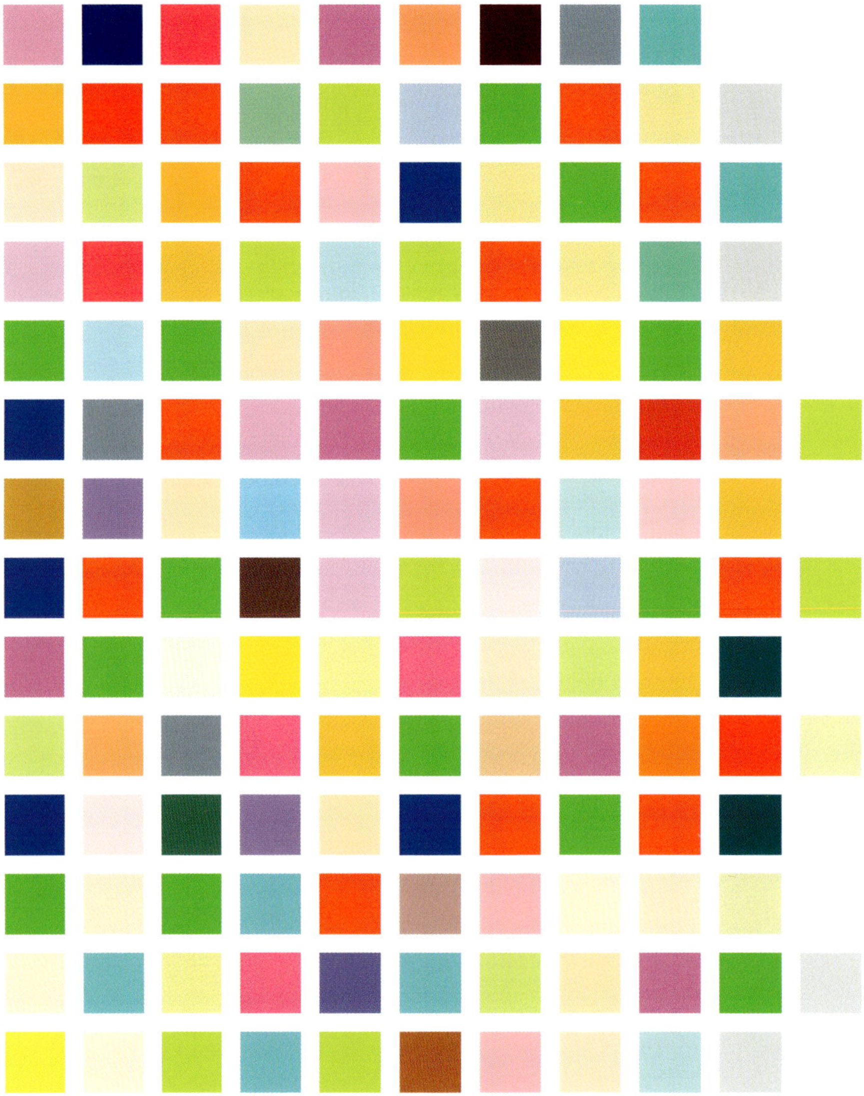

6.

7.

8.

9.

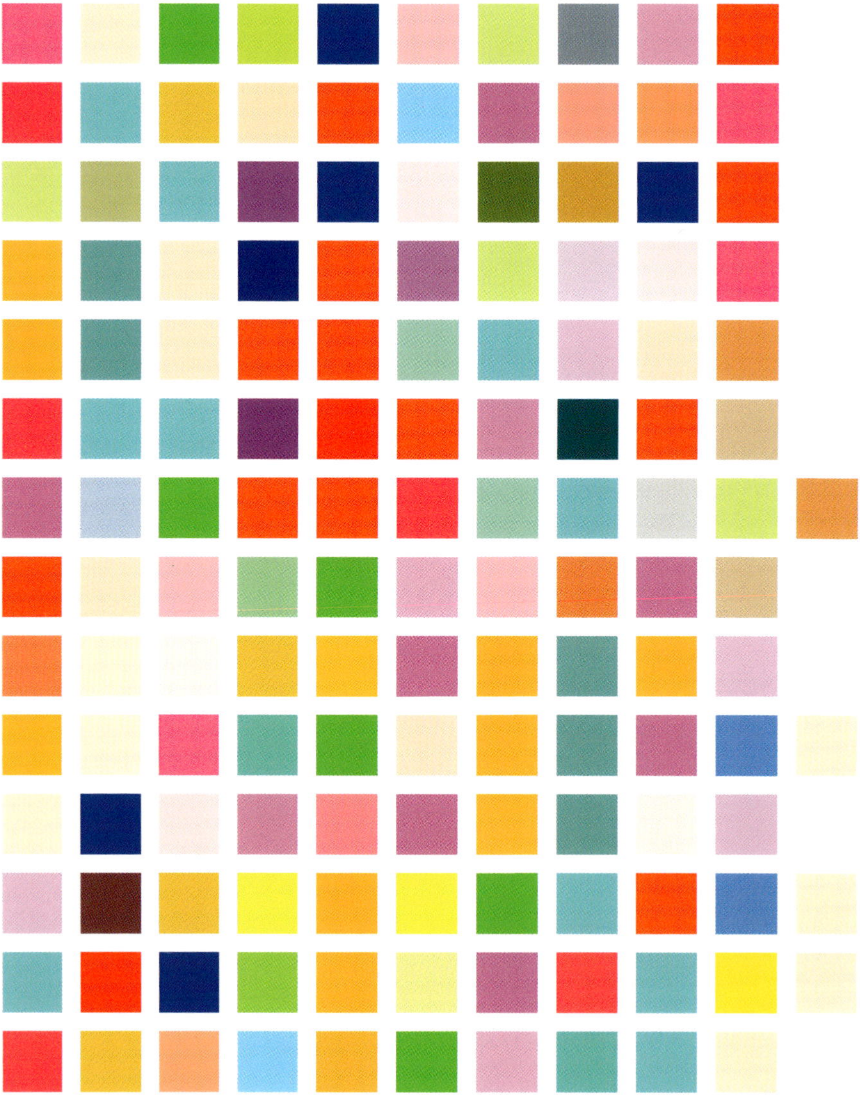

10.

11.

12.

13.

14.

15.

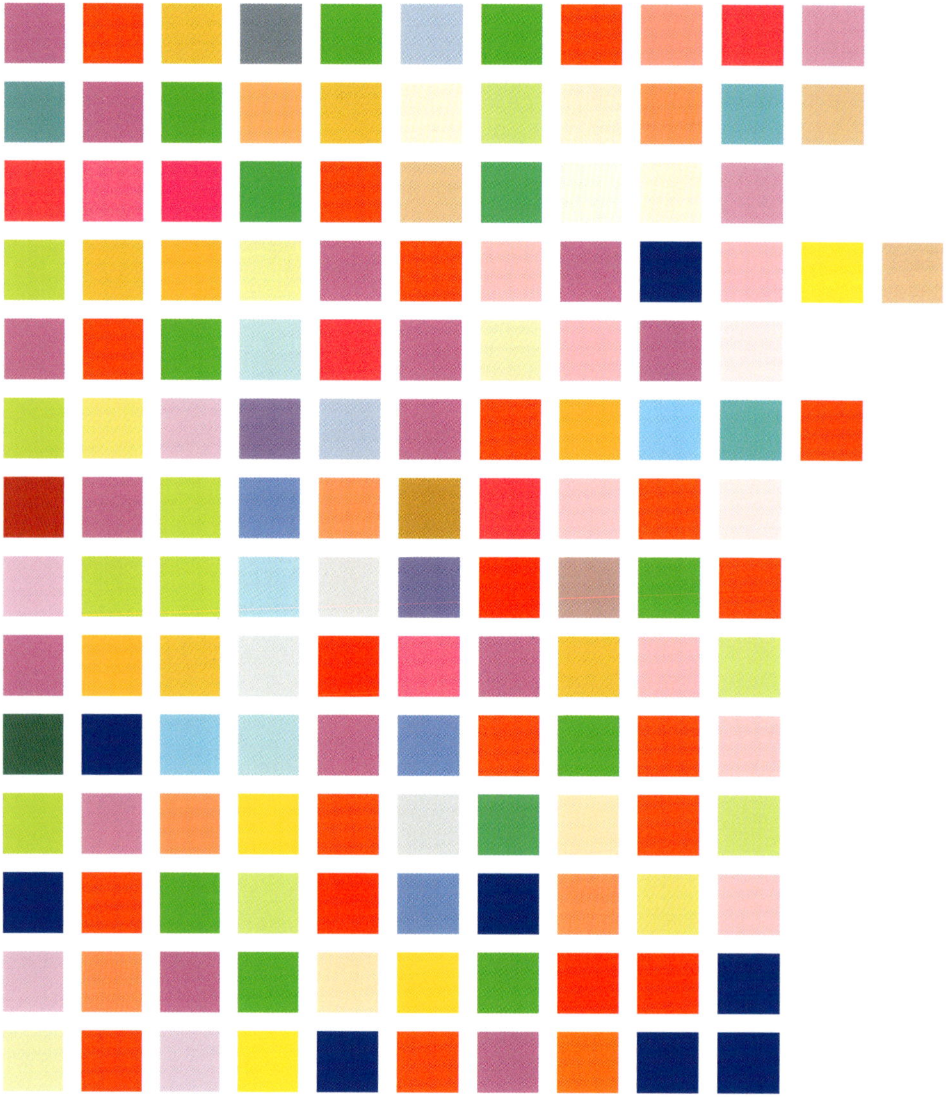

16.

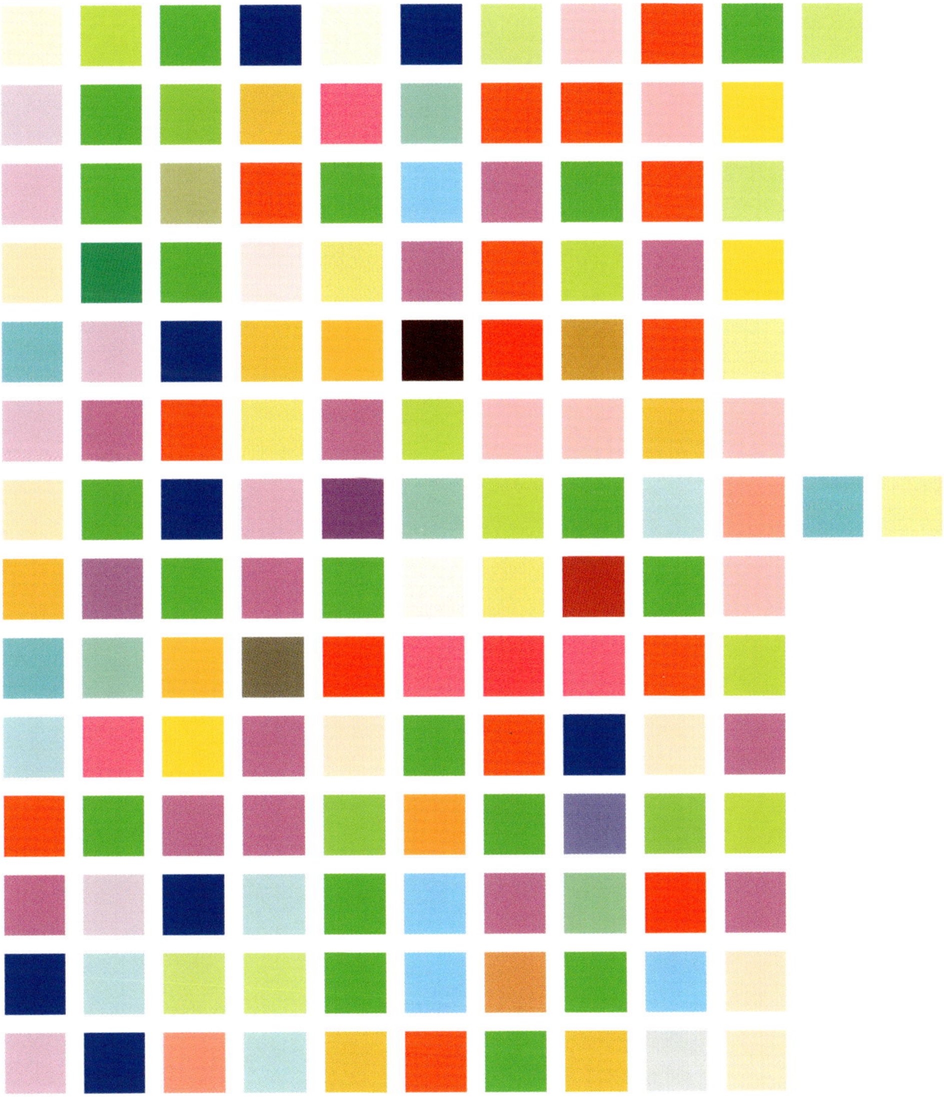

17.

18.

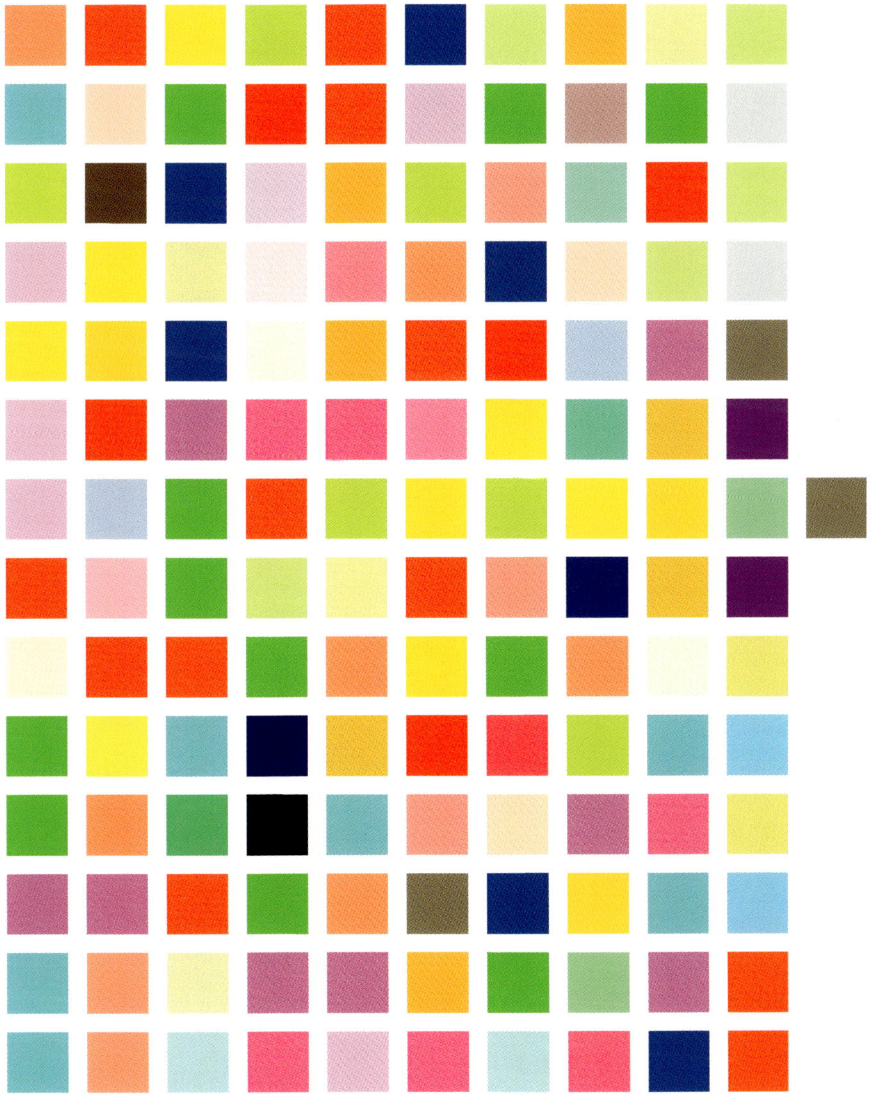

19.

20.

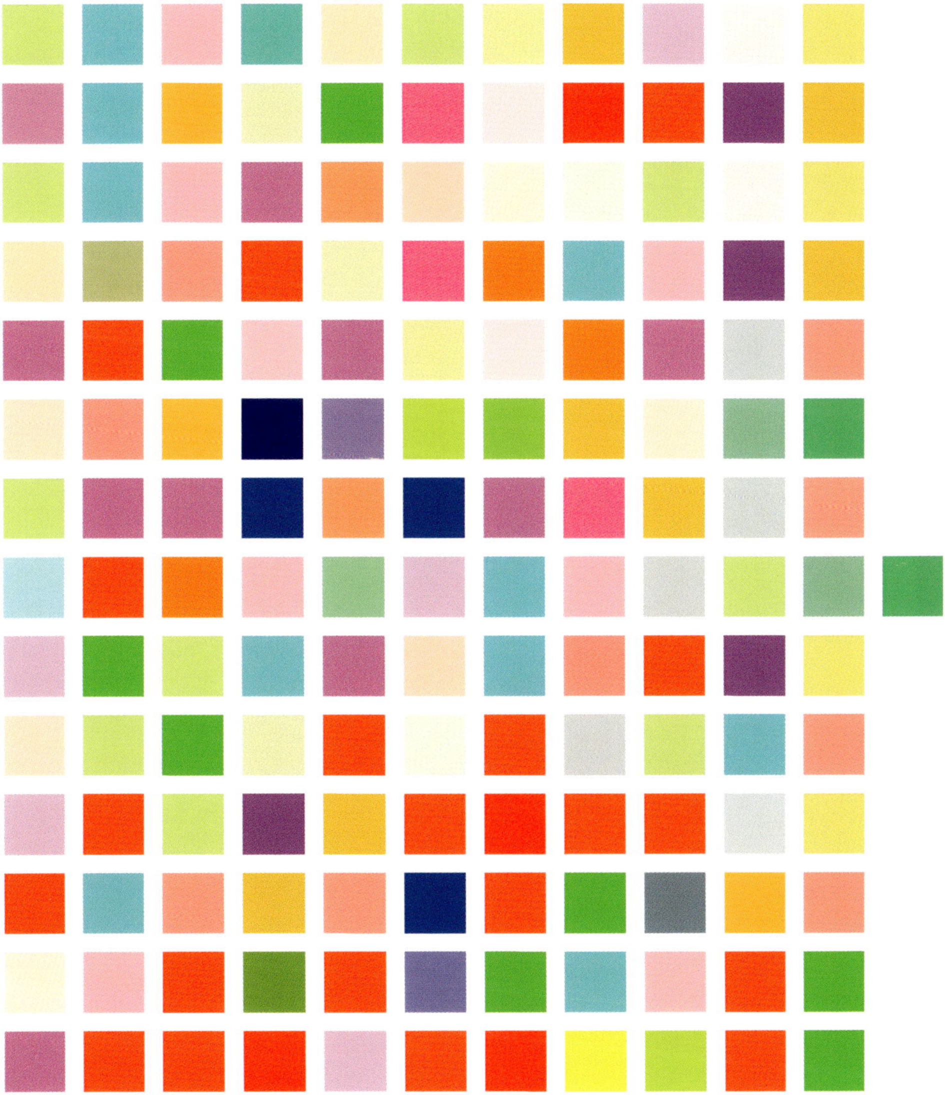

21.

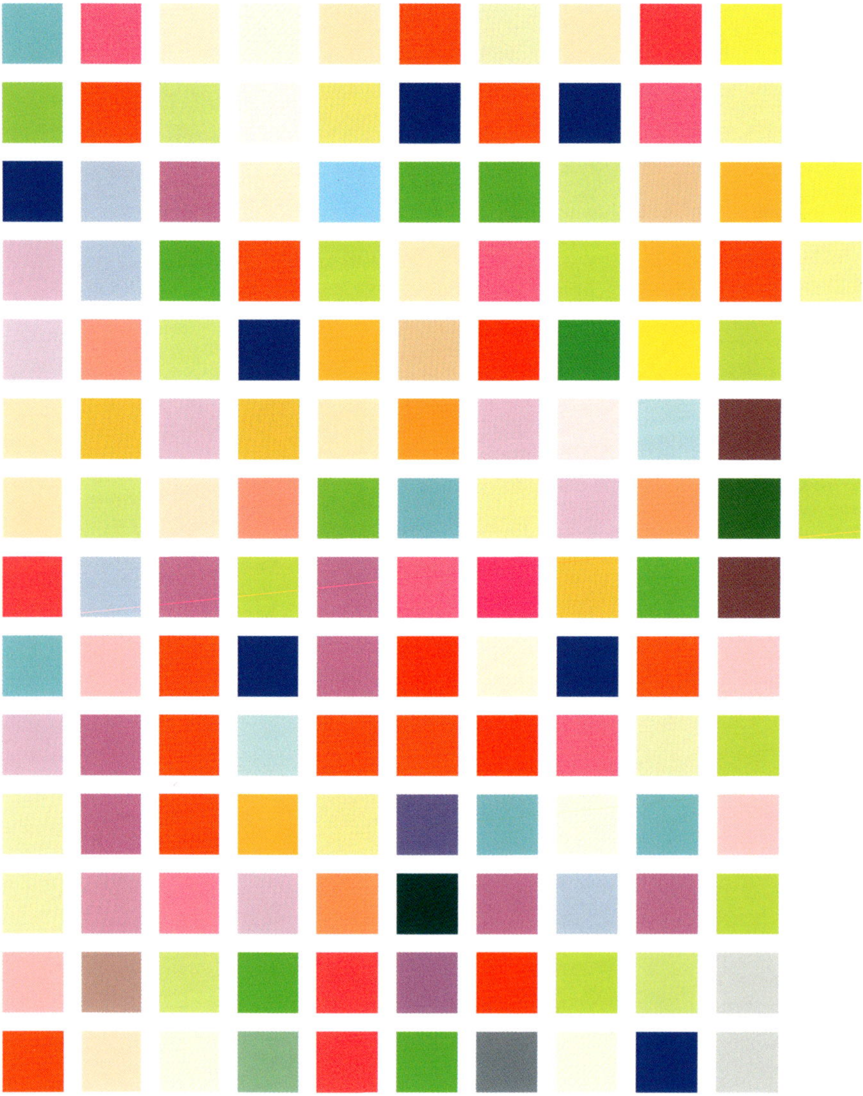

22.

23.

24.

25.

26.

27.

28.

29.

30.

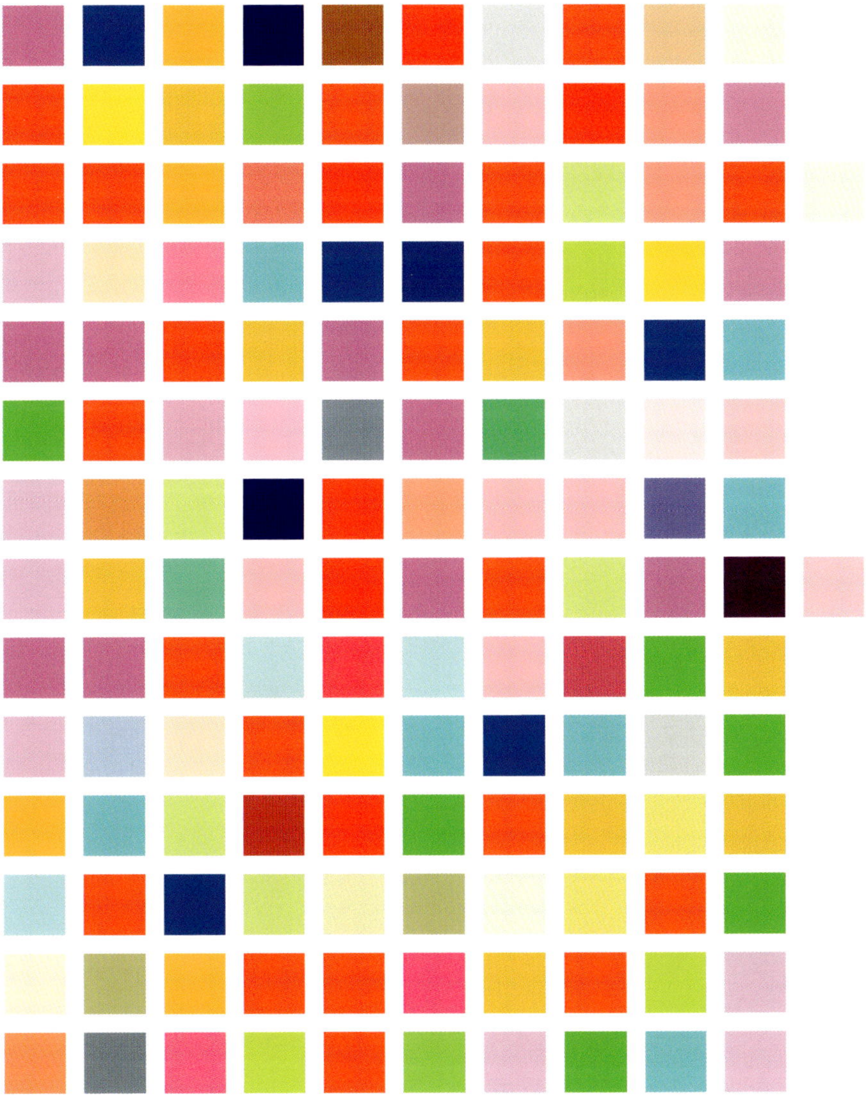

31.

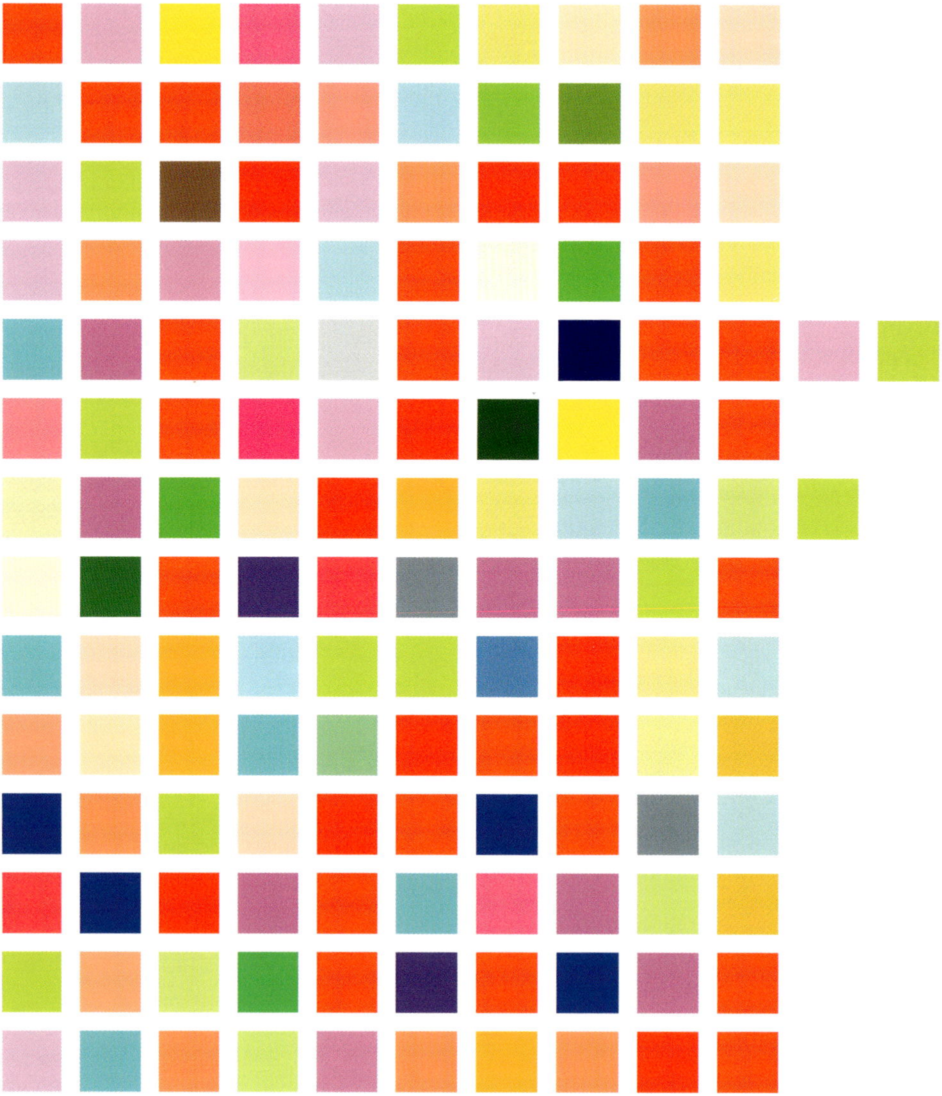

32.

33.

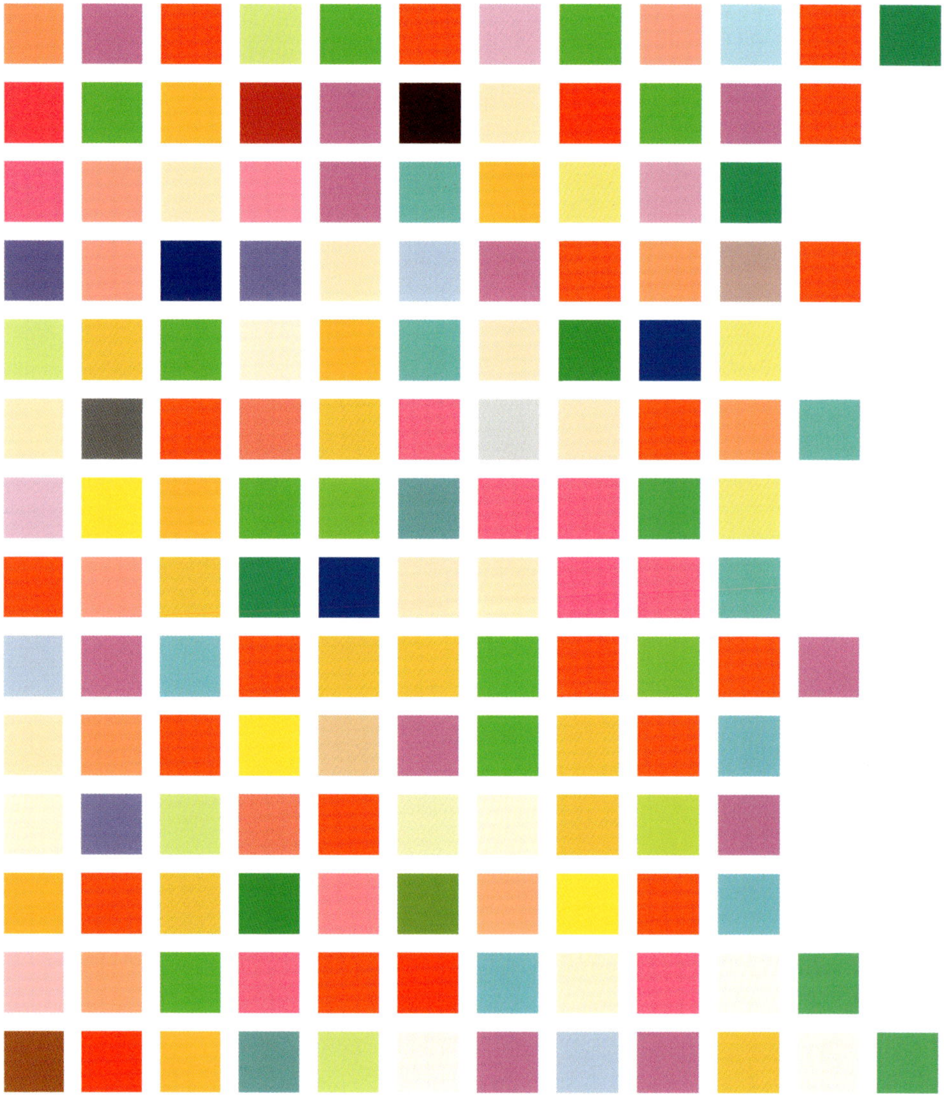

34.

35.

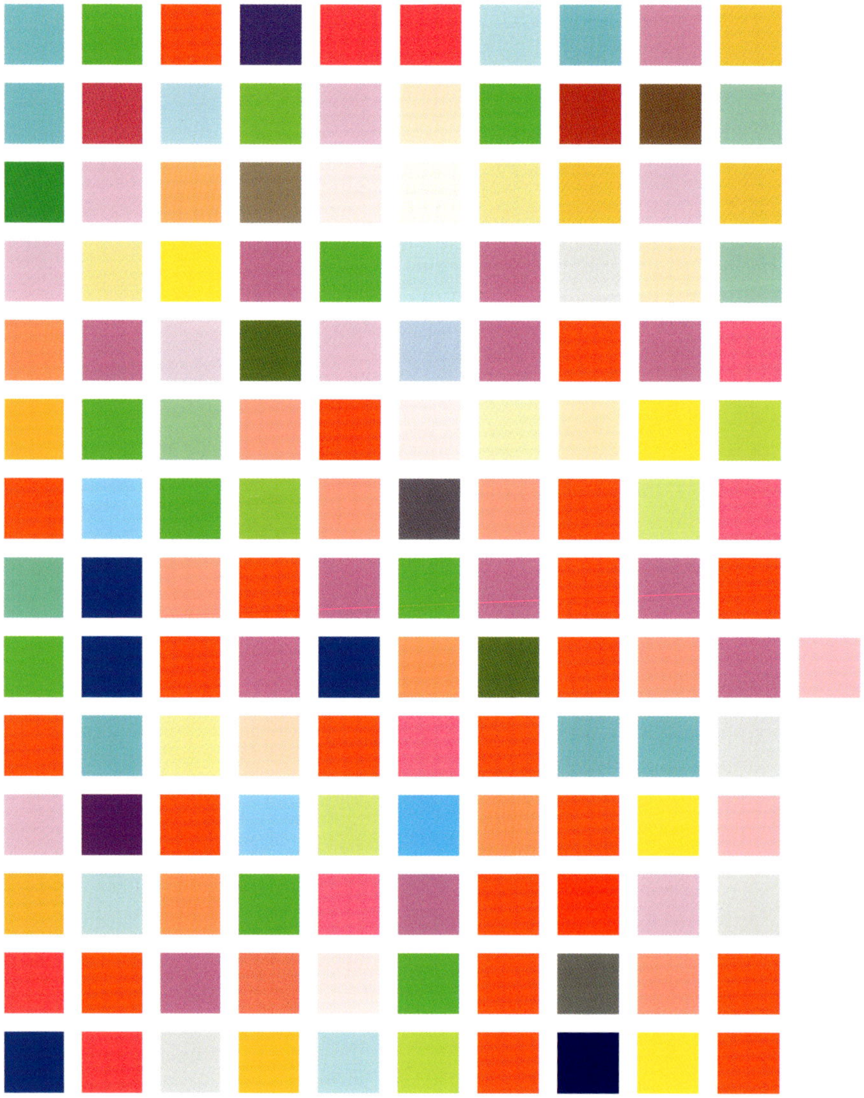

36.

37.

38.

39.

40.

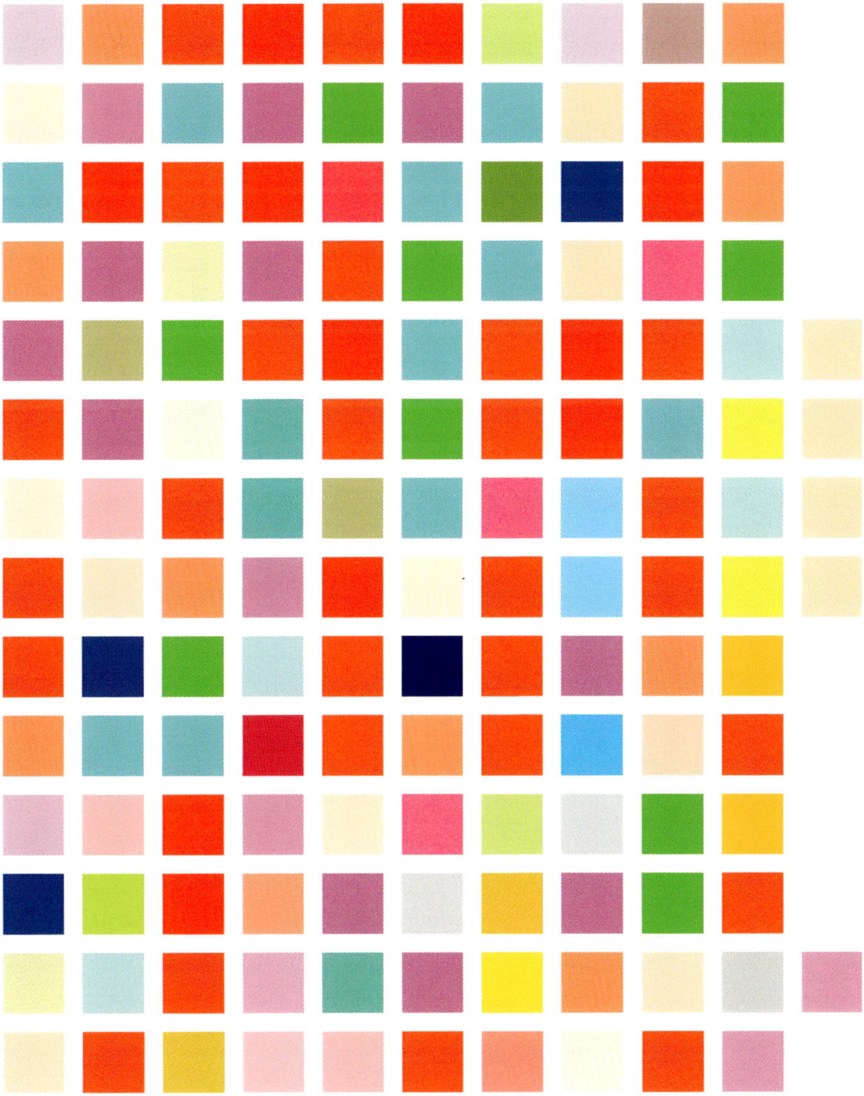

41.

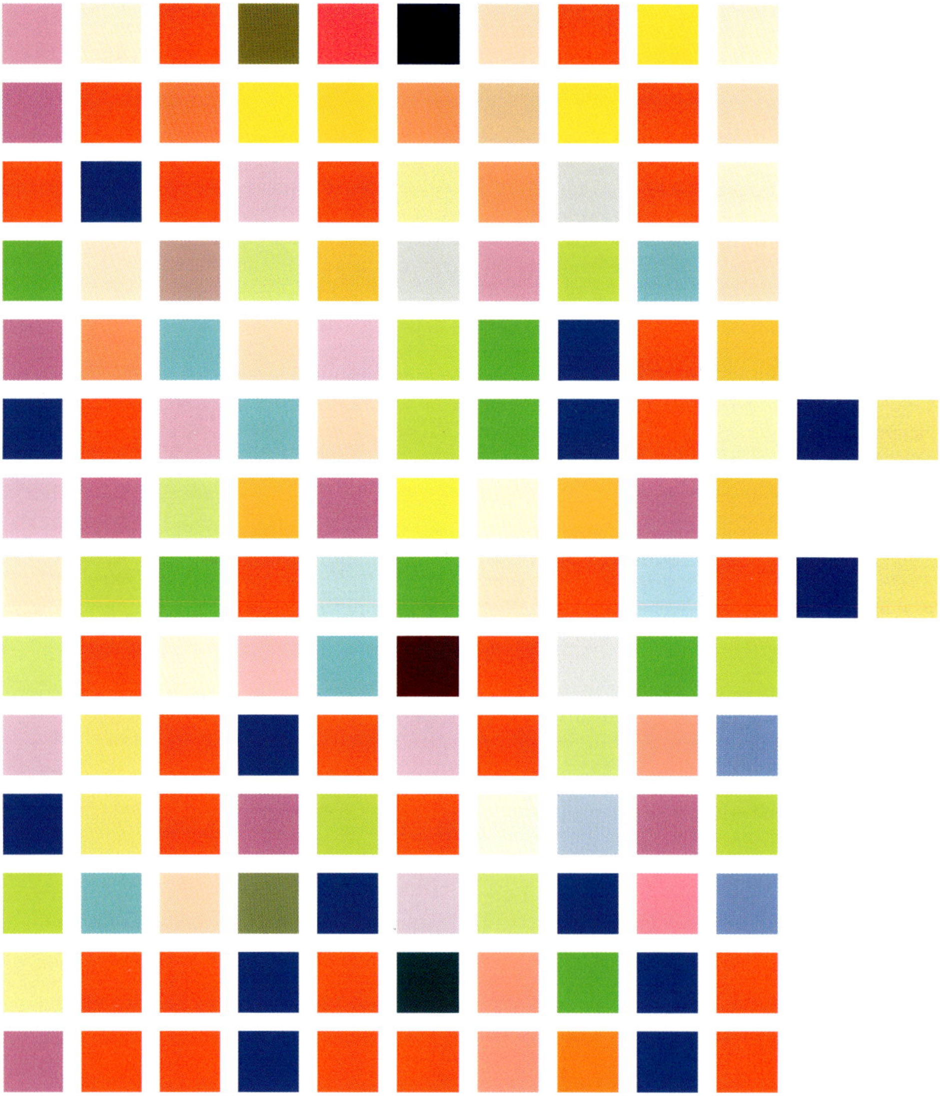

42.

43.

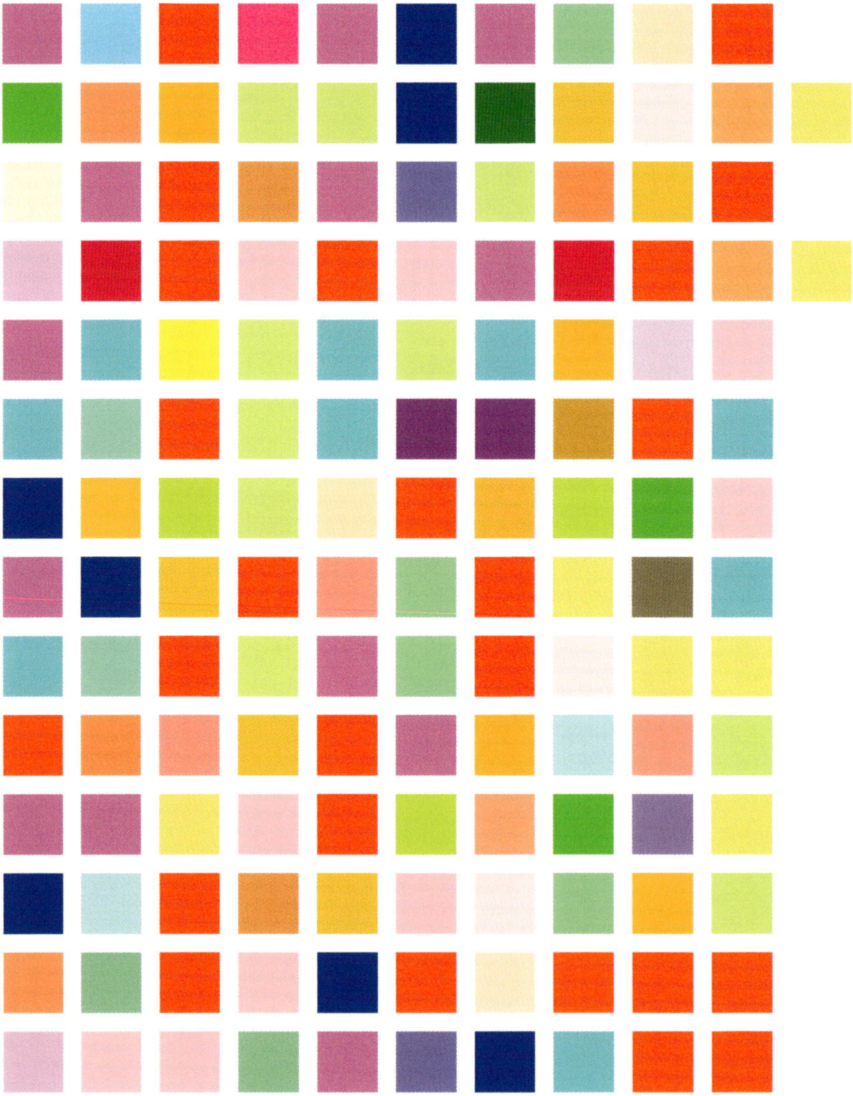

44.

45.

46.

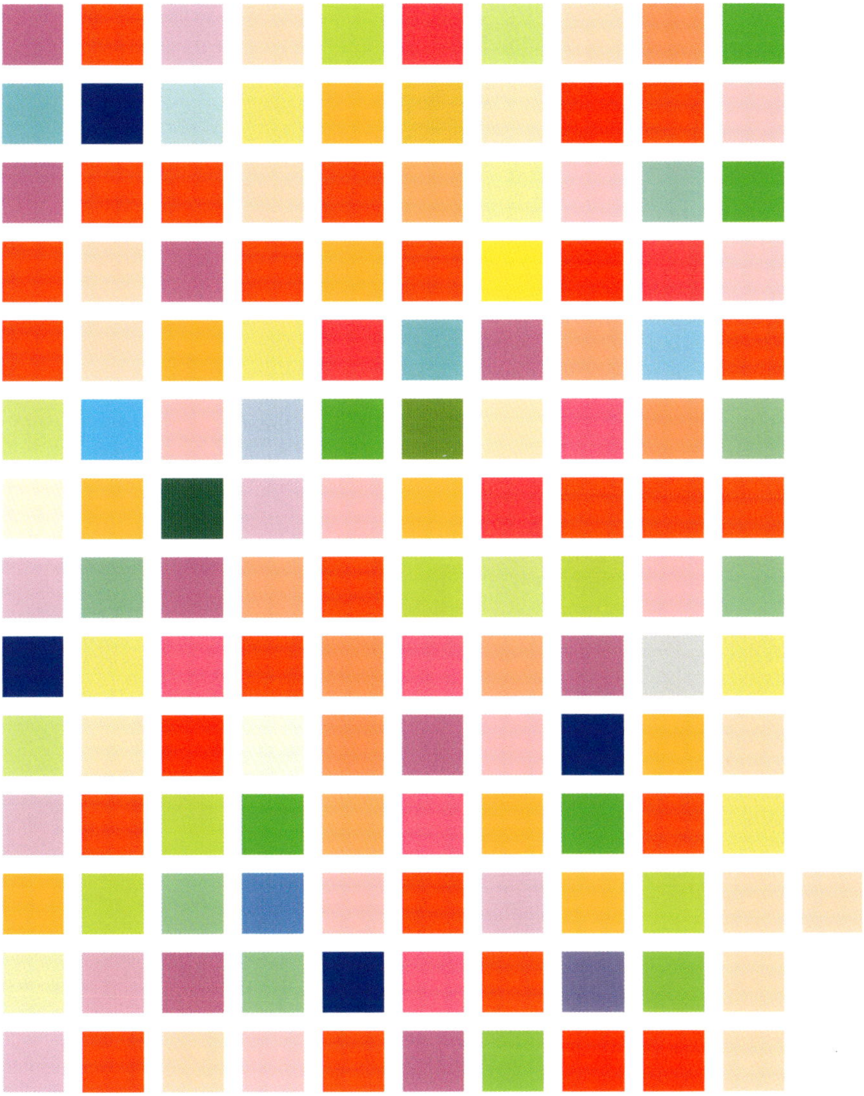

47.

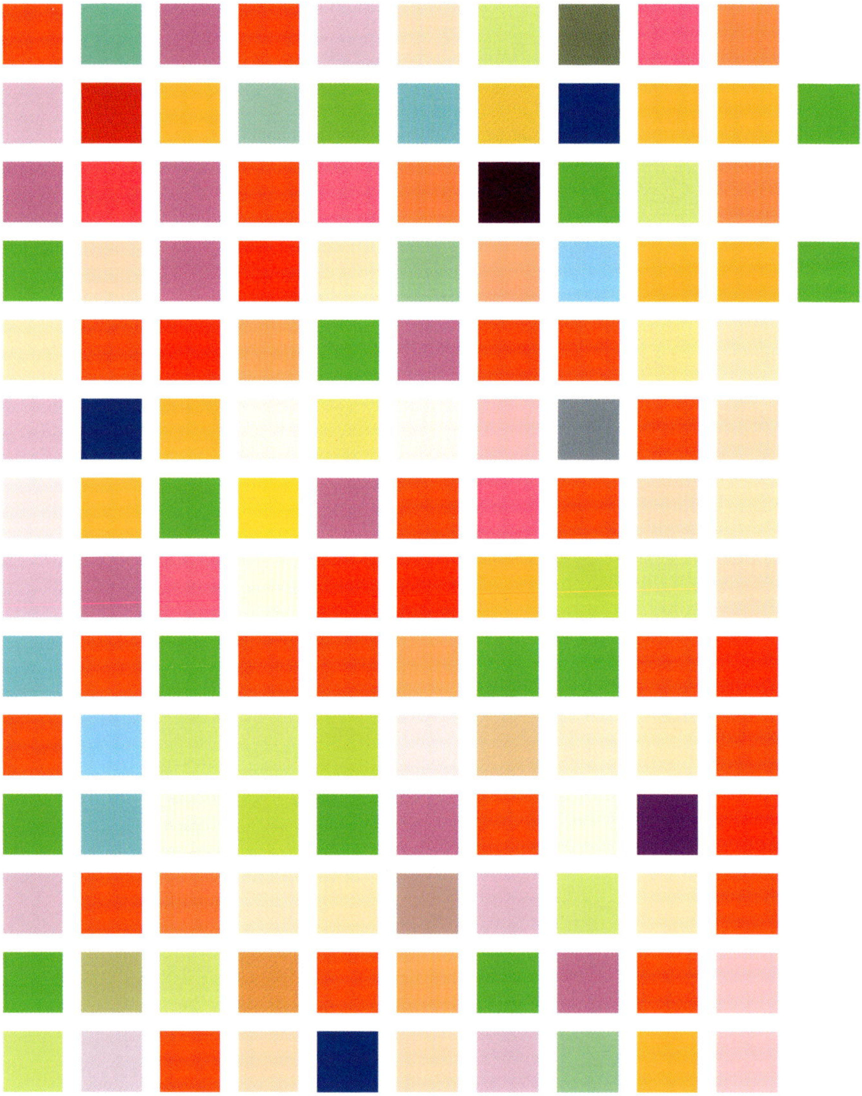

48.

49.

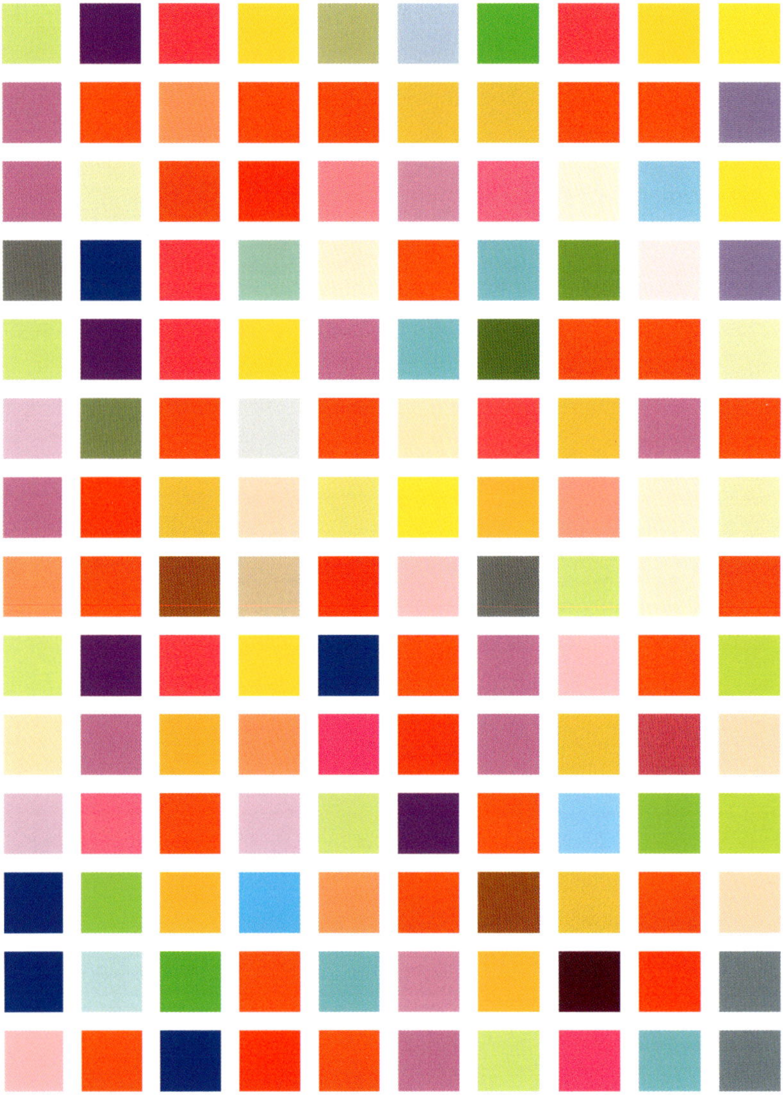

50.

51.

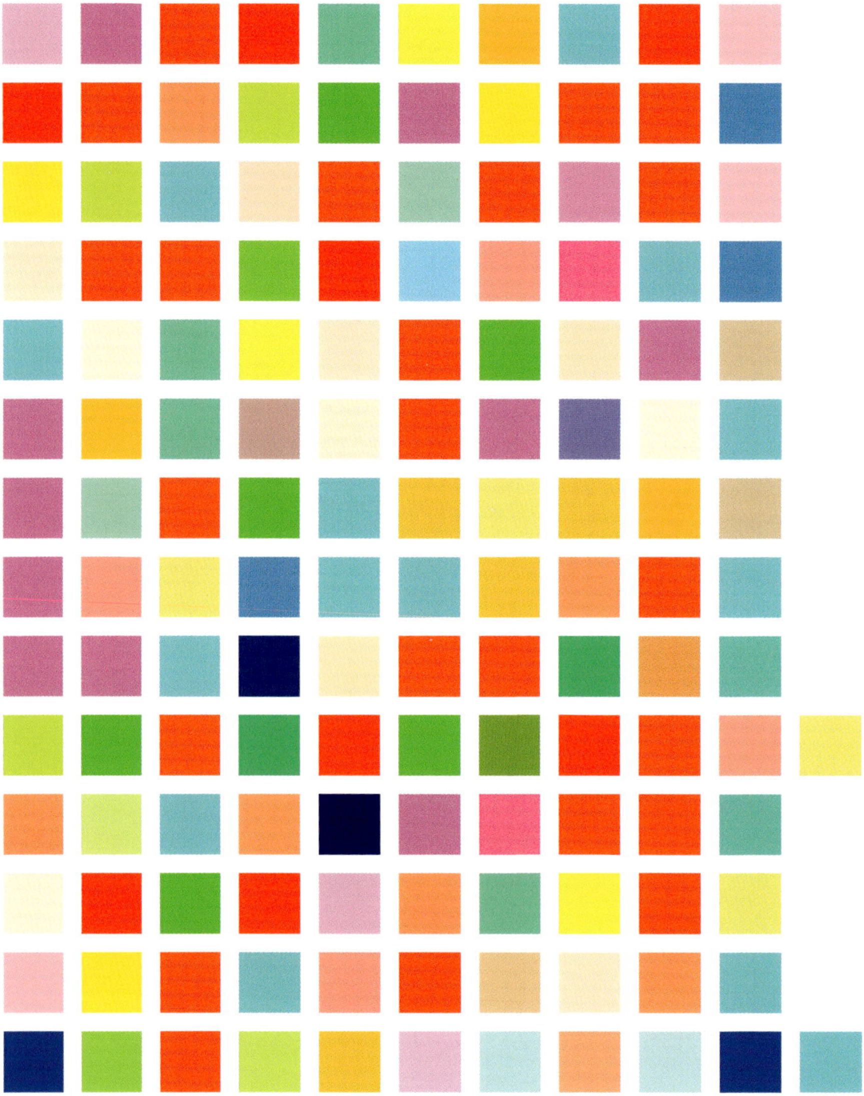

52.

53.

54.

55.

56.

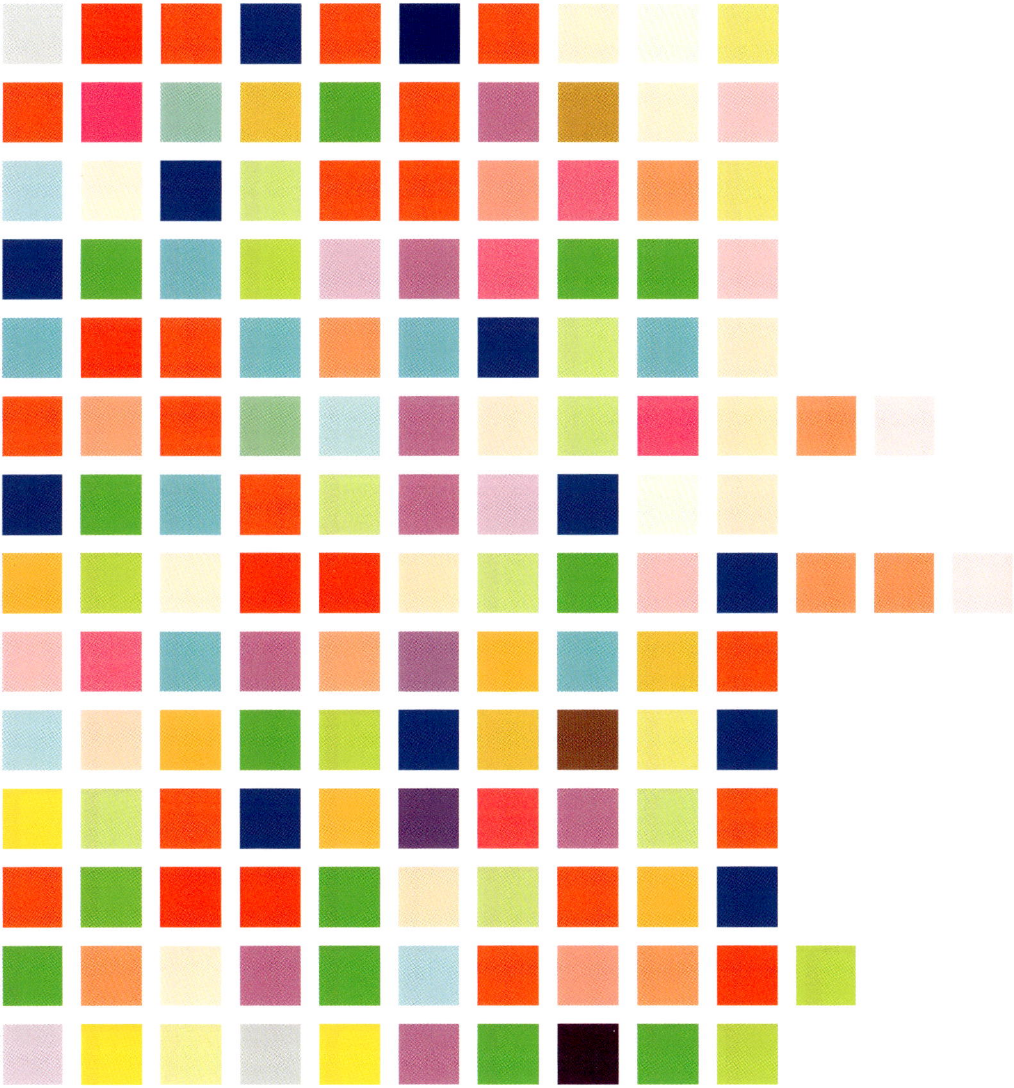

57.

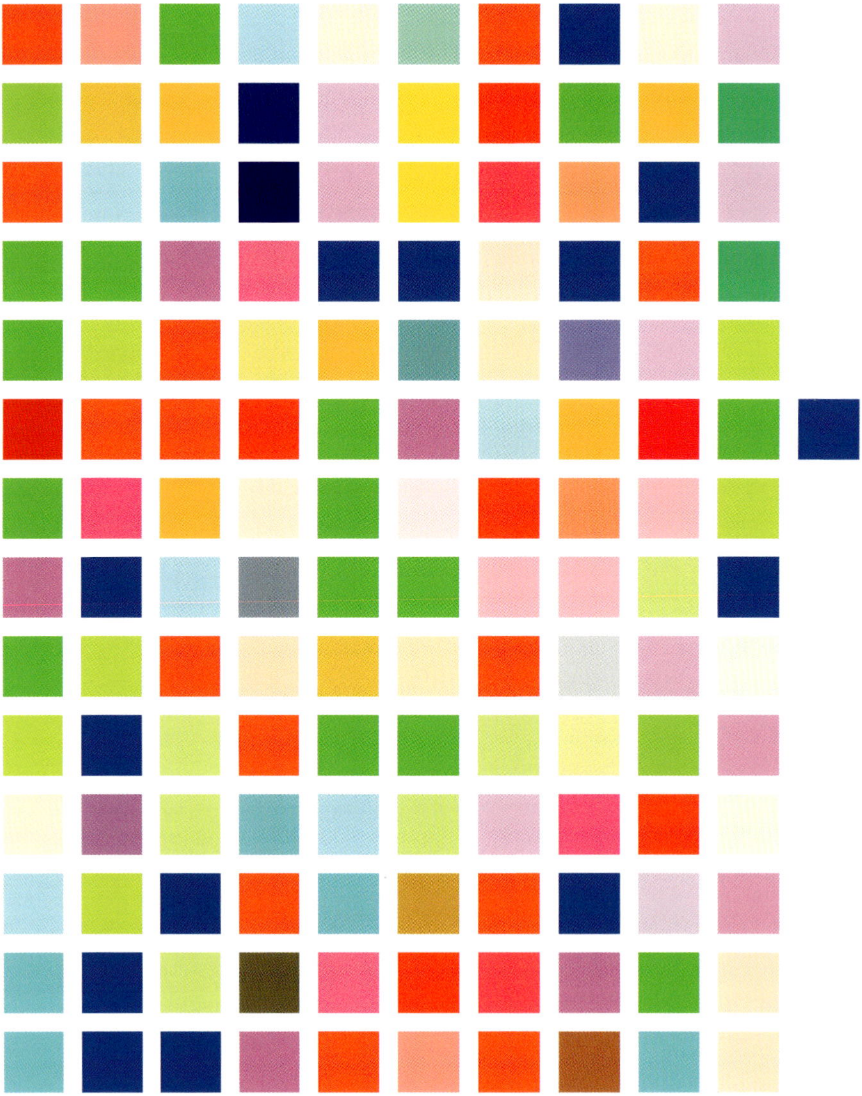

58.

59.

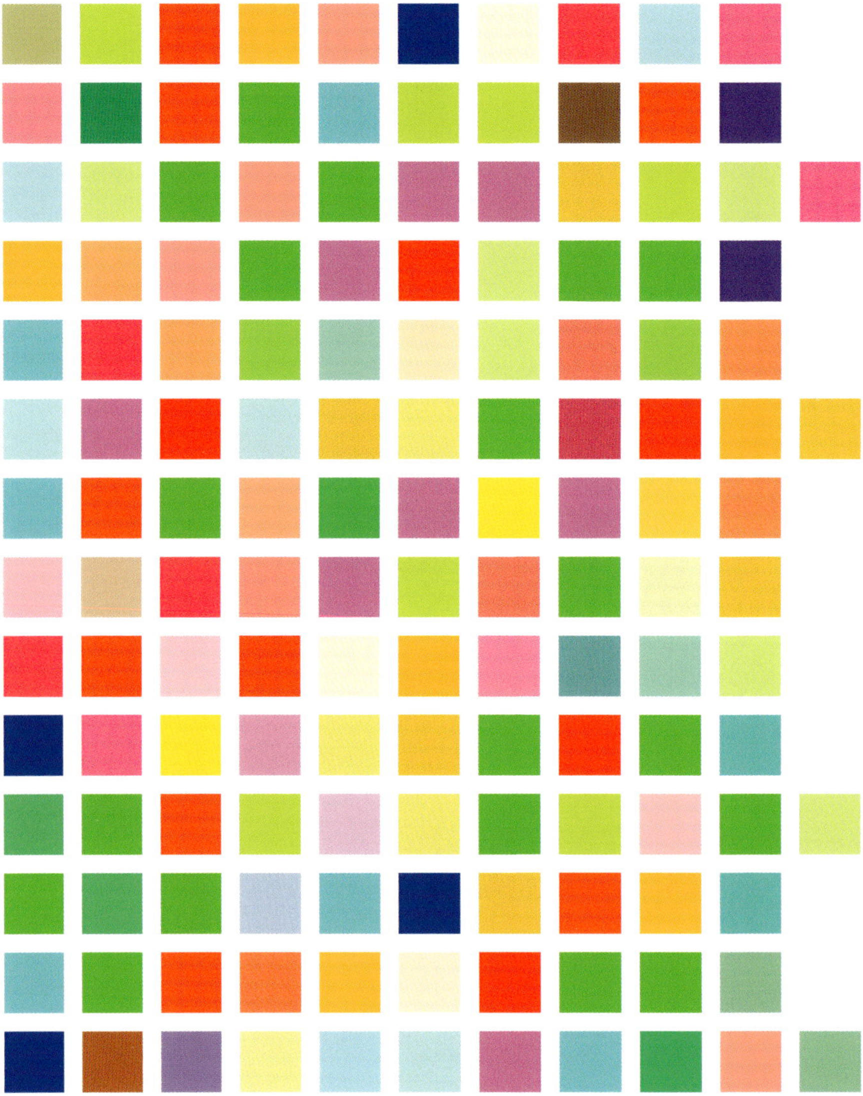

60.

61.

62.

63.

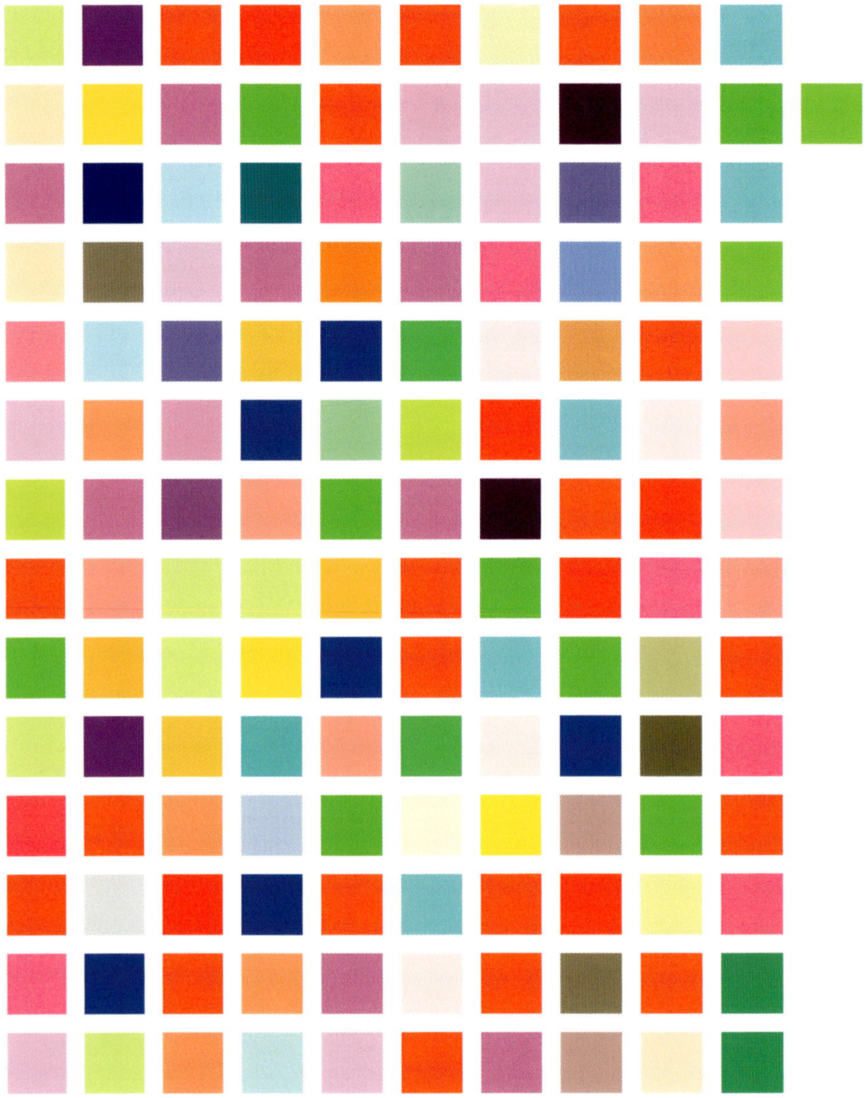

64.

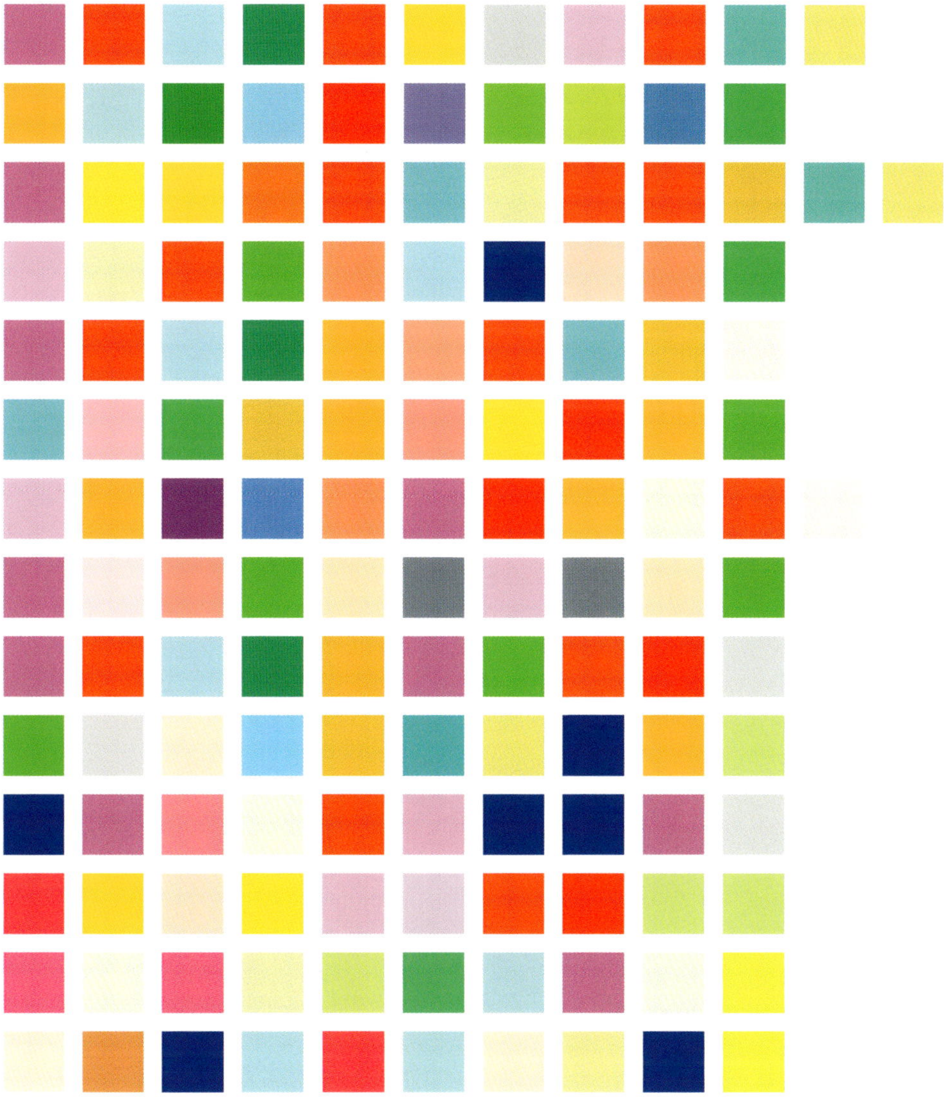

65.

66.

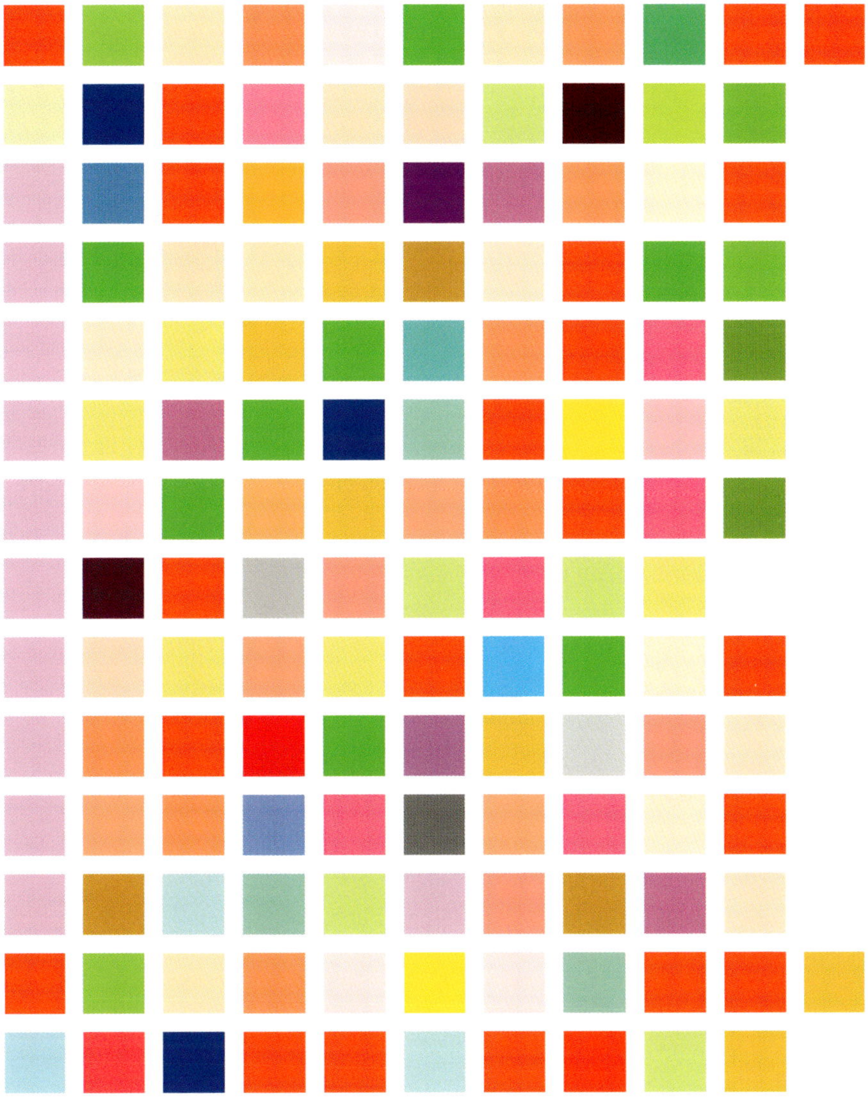

67.

68.

69.

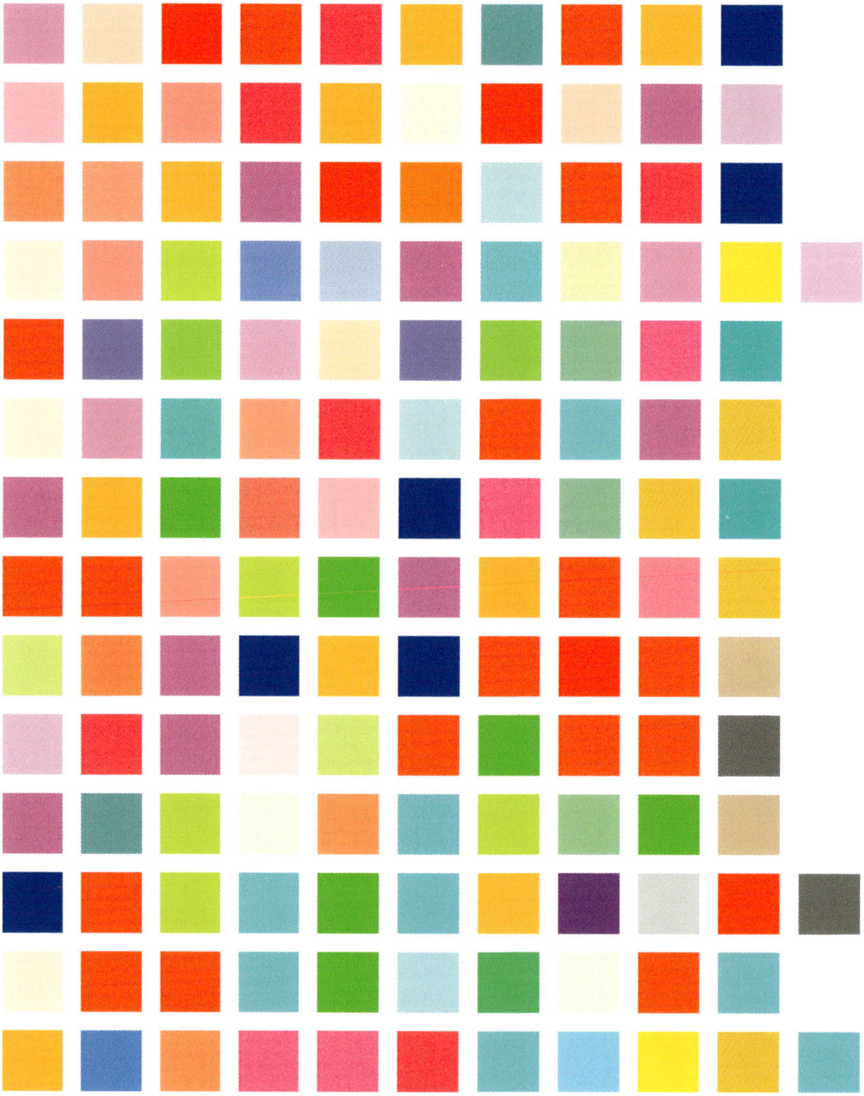

70.

71.

72.

73.

74.

75.

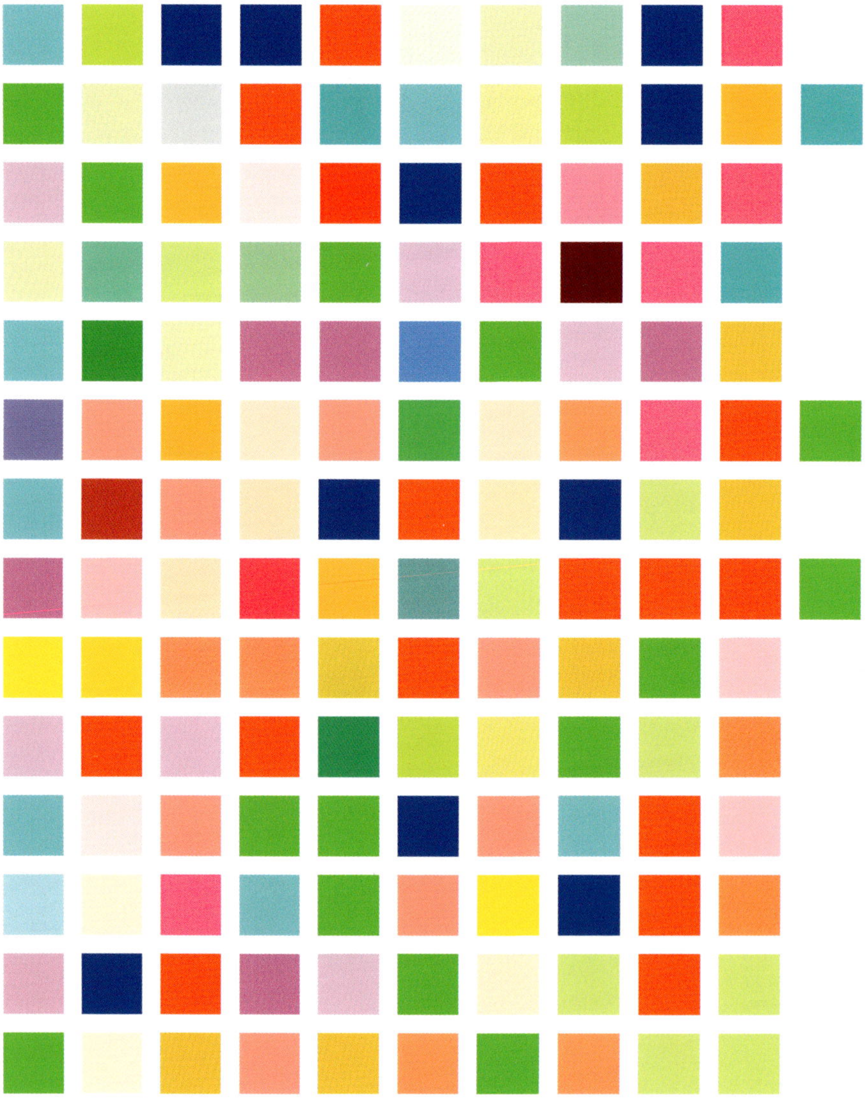

76.

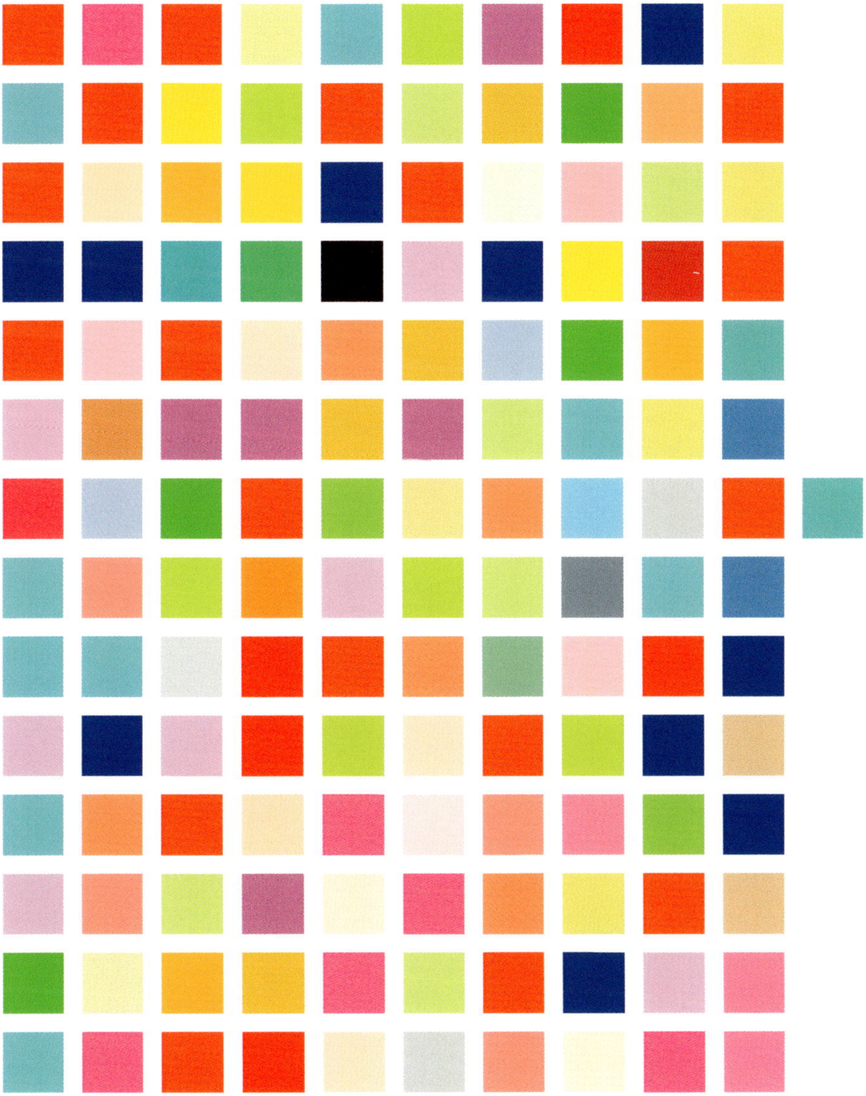

77.

78.

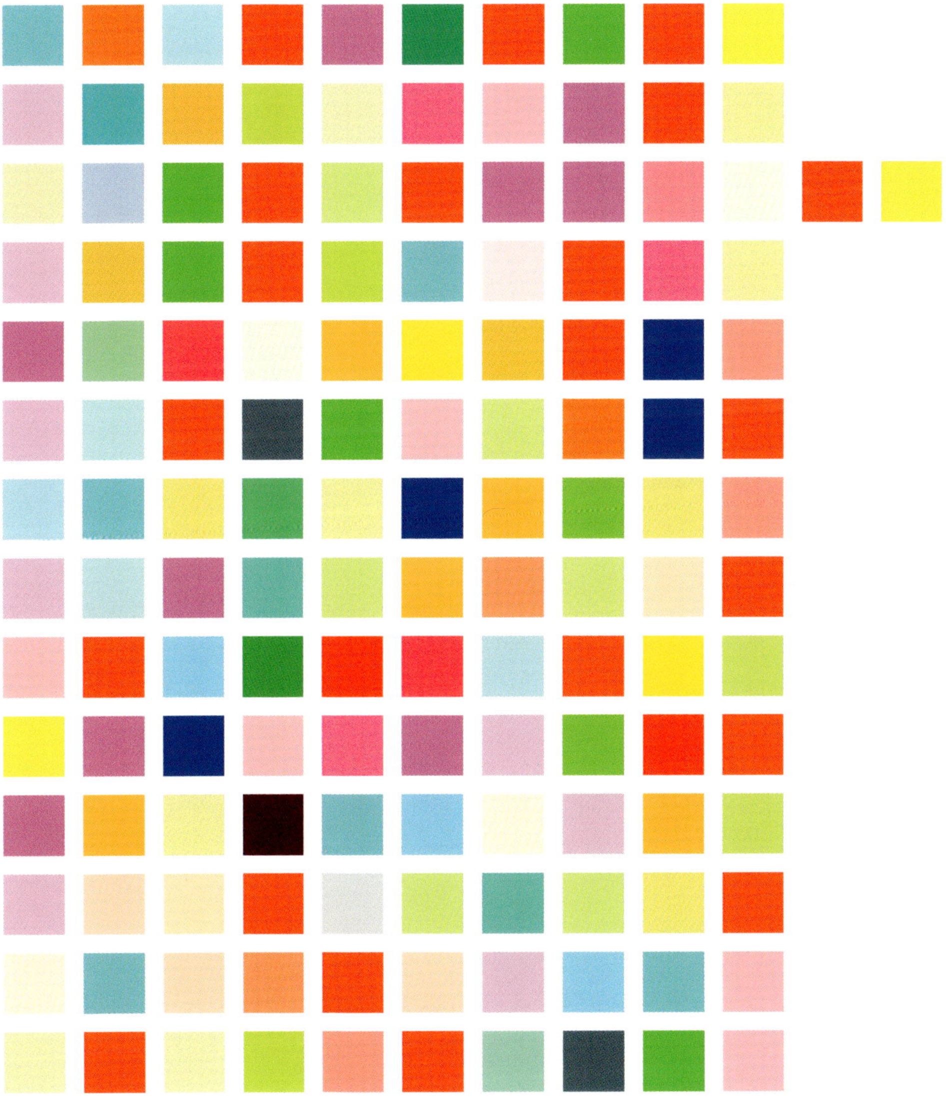

79.

80.

81.

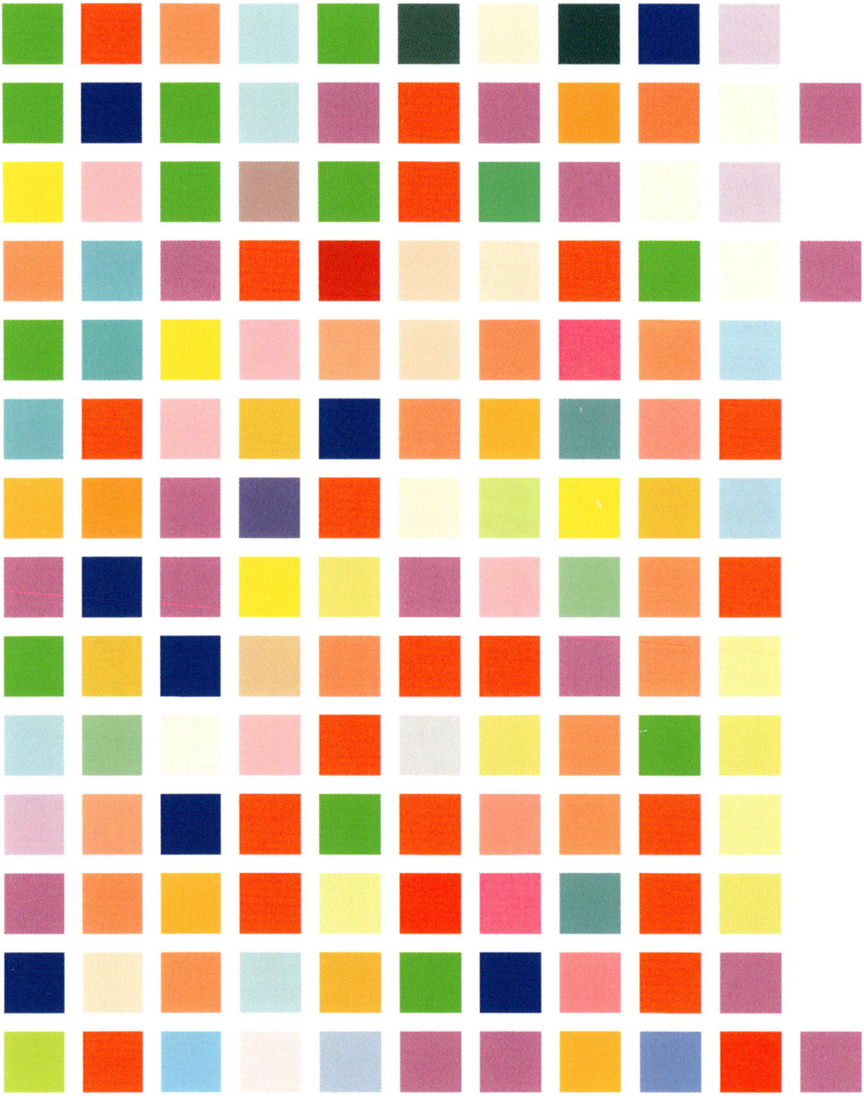

82.

83.

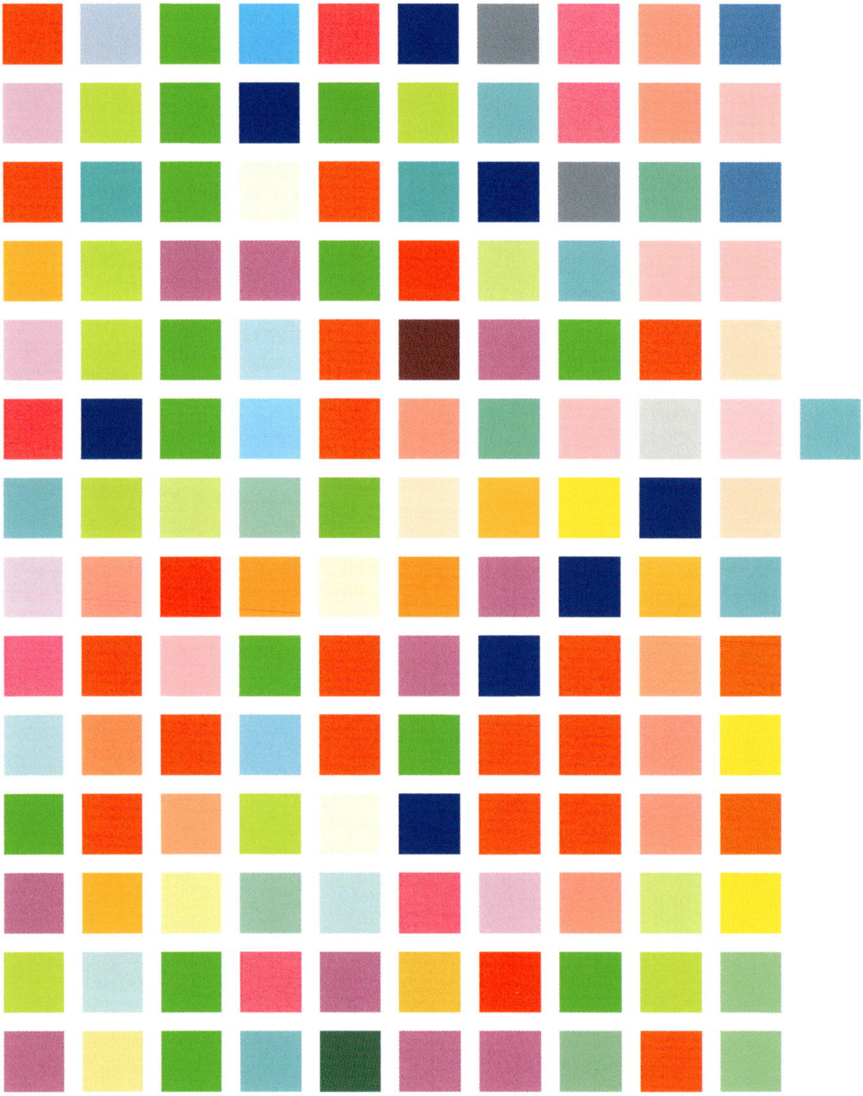

84.

85.

86.

87.

88.

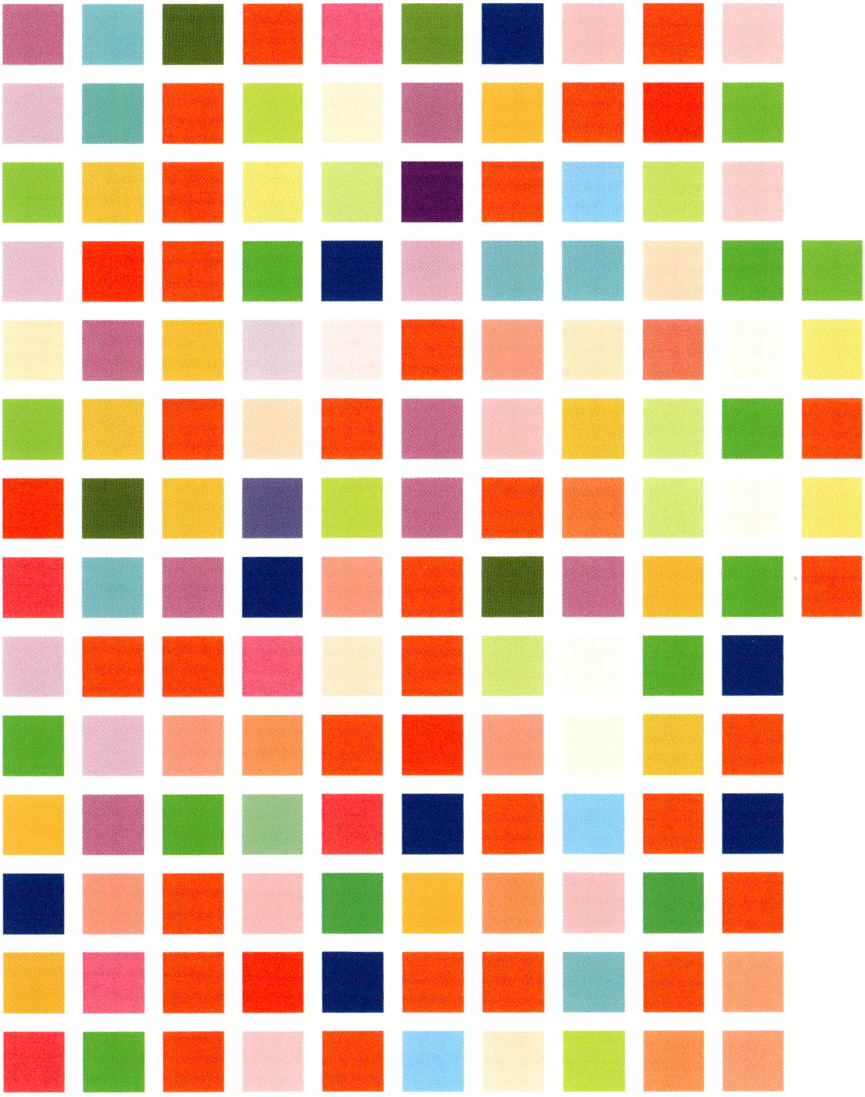

89.

90.

91.

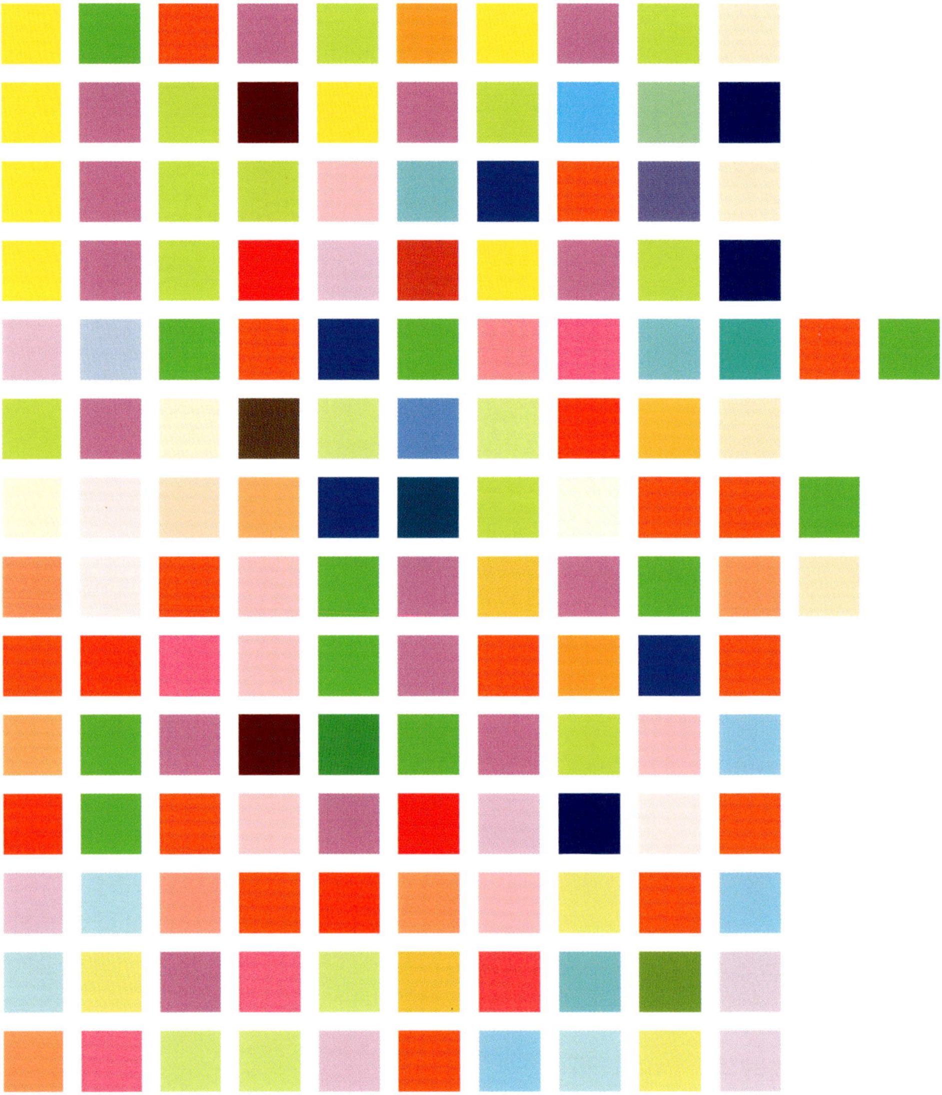

92.

93.

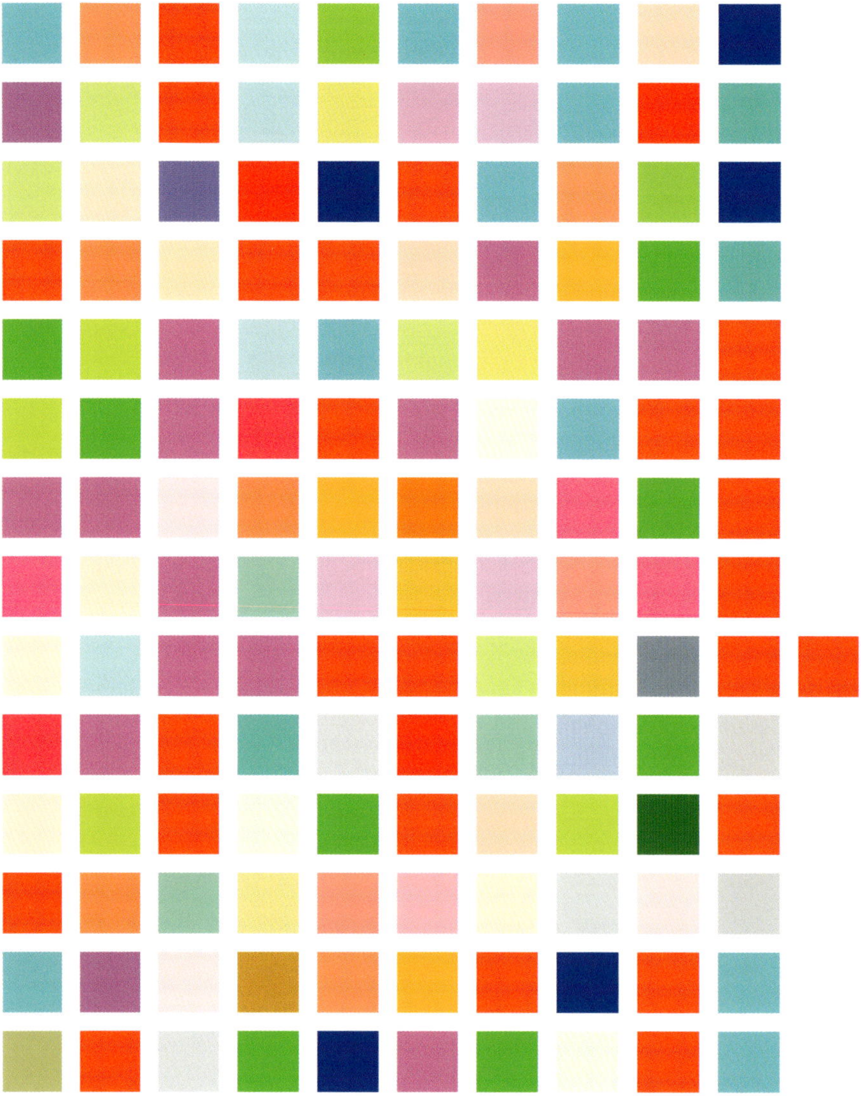

94.

95.

96.

97.

98.

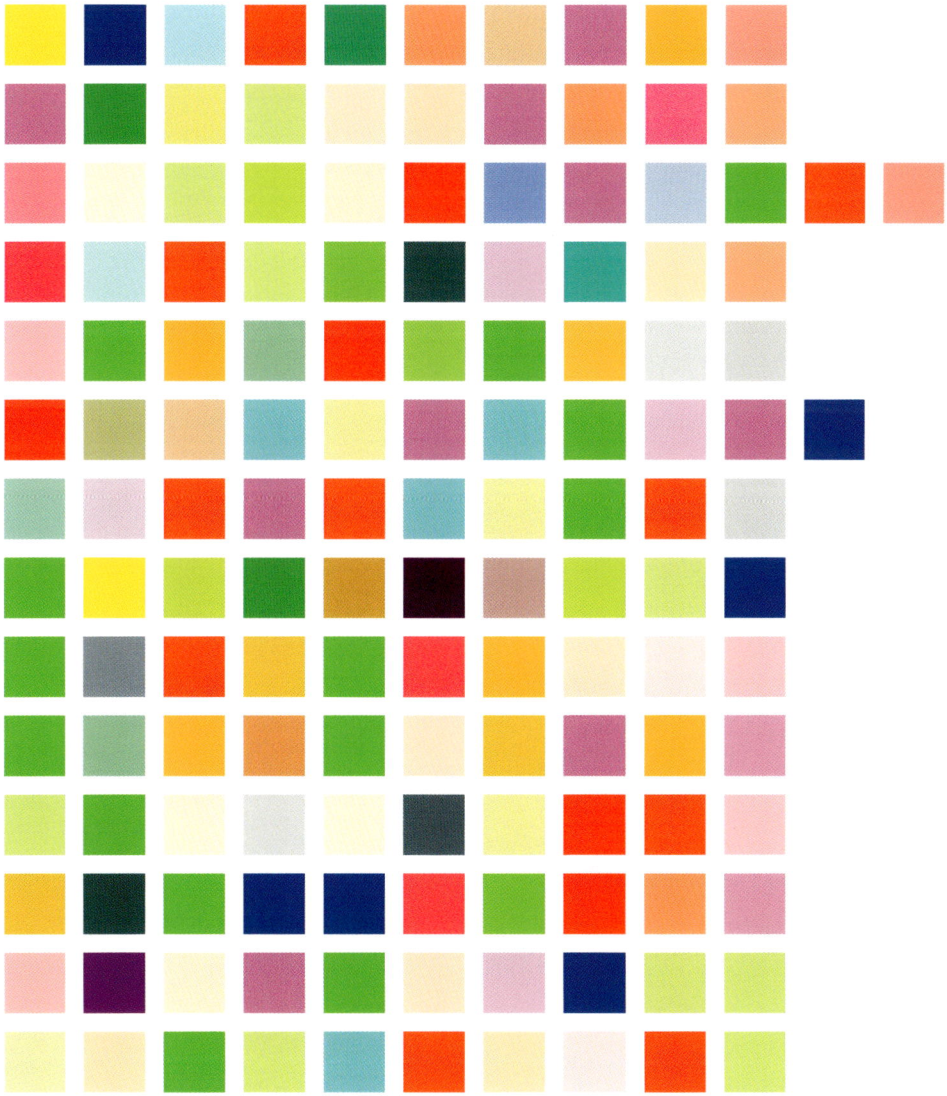

99.

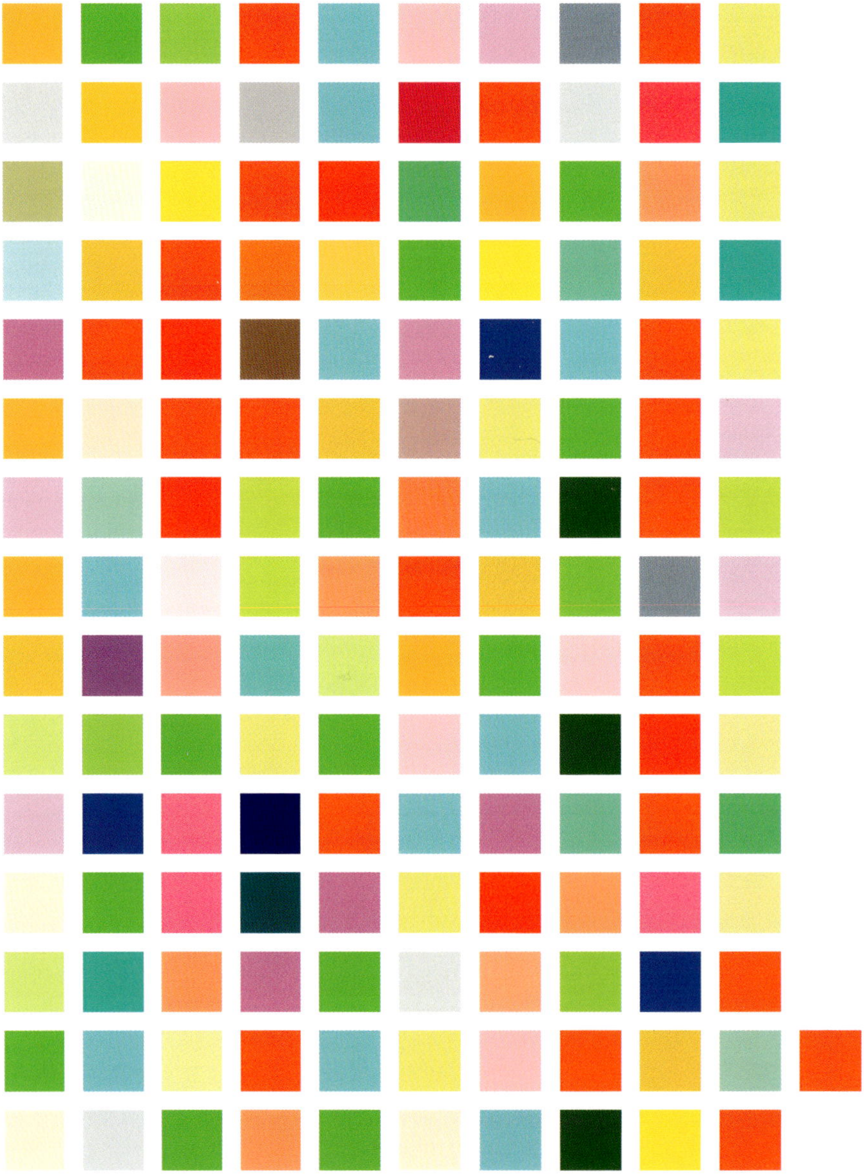

100.

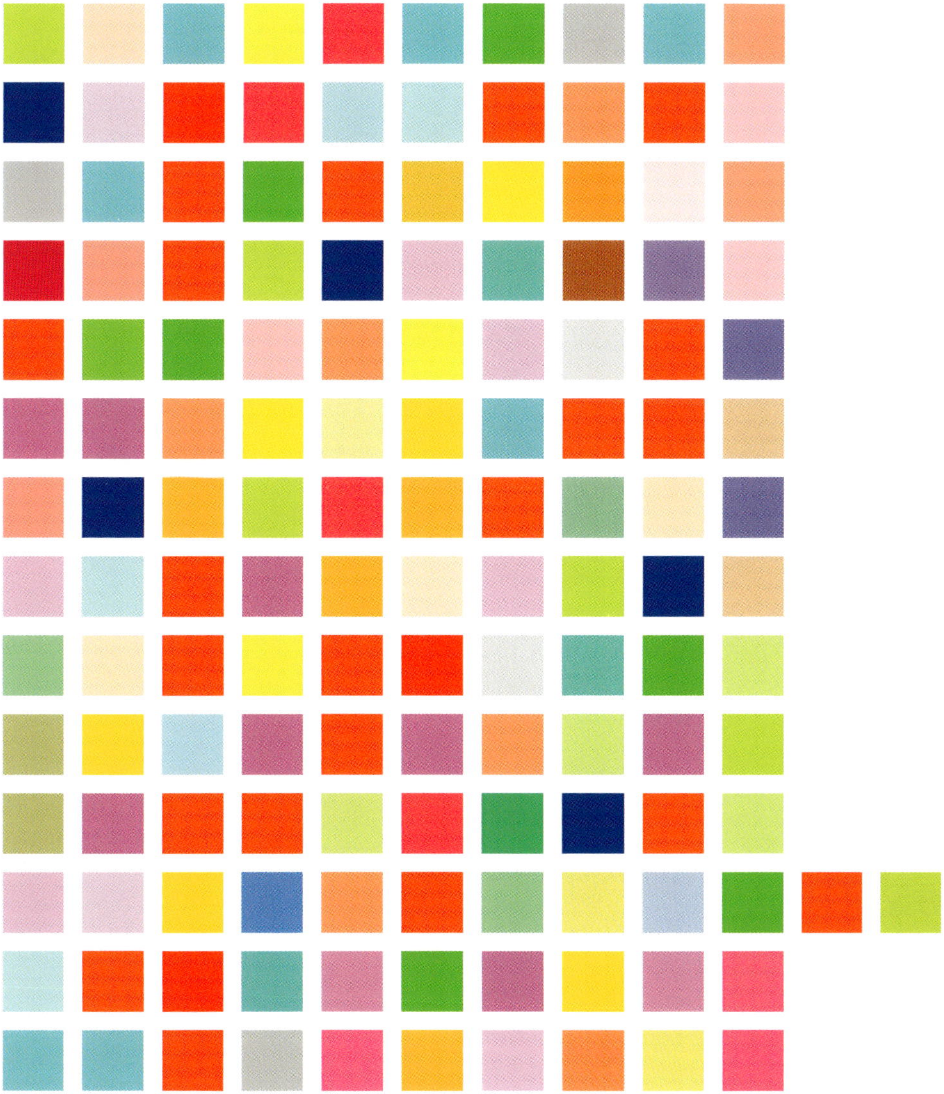

101.

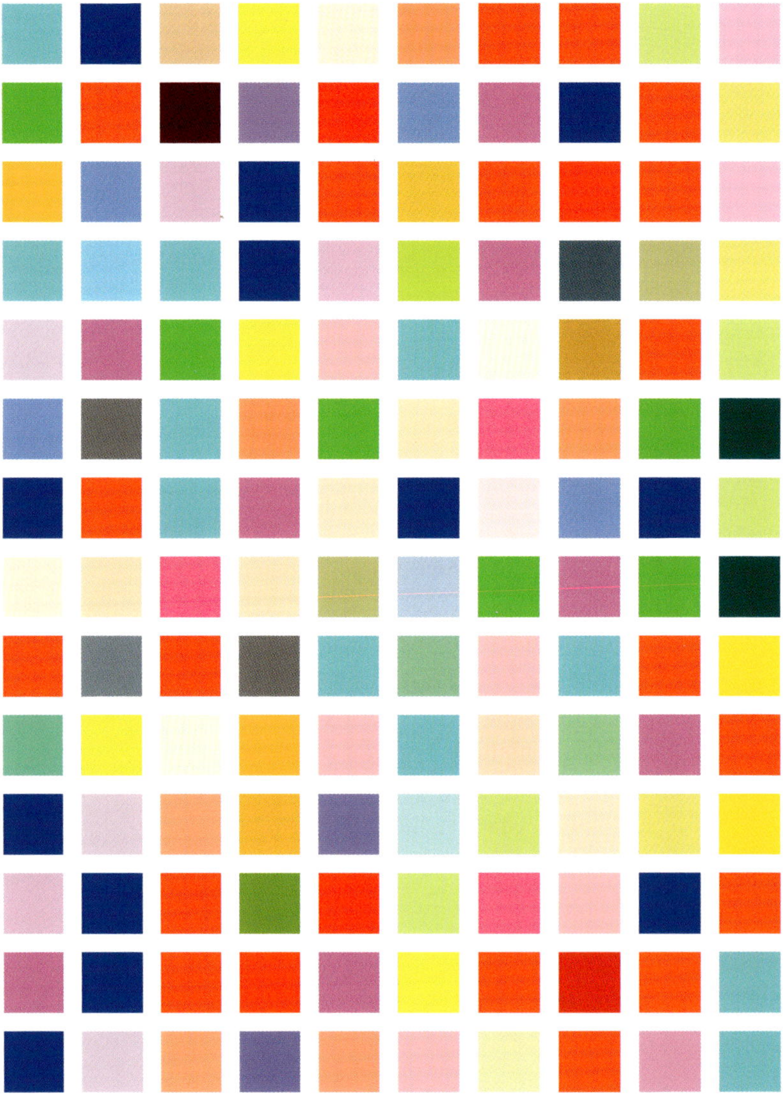

102.

103.

104.

105.

106.

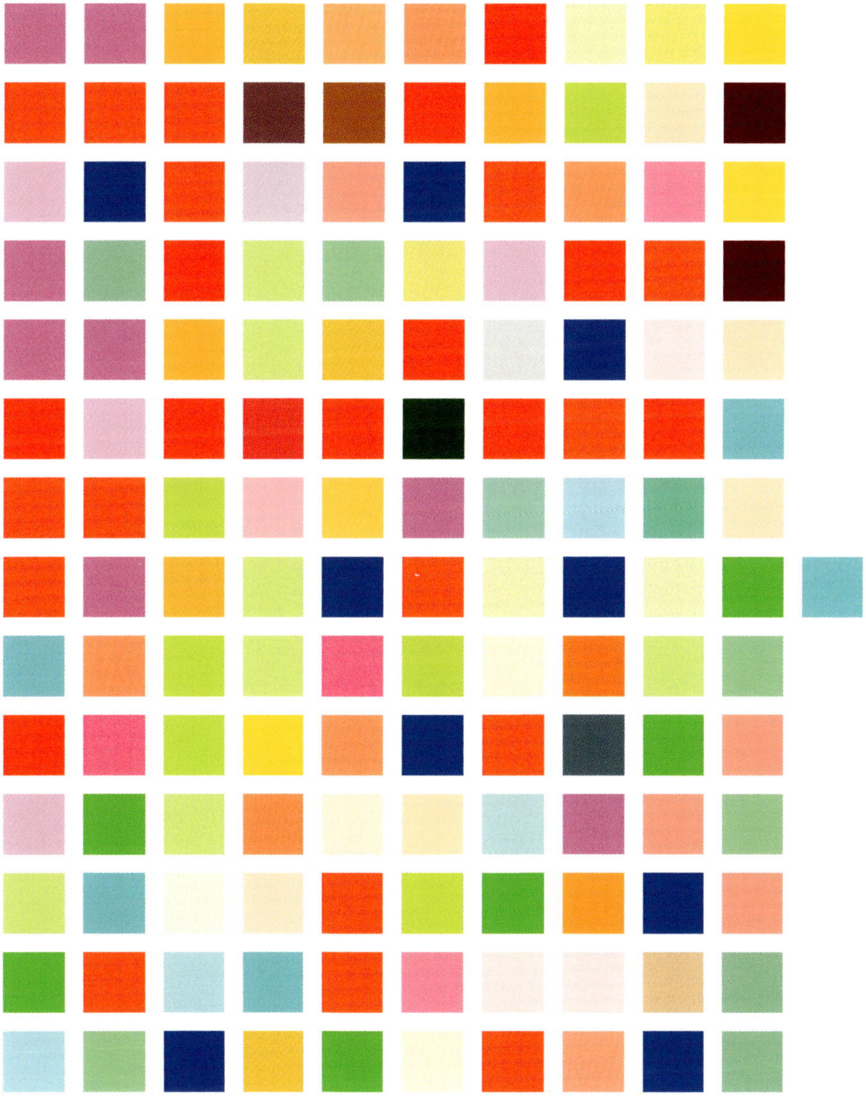

107.

108.

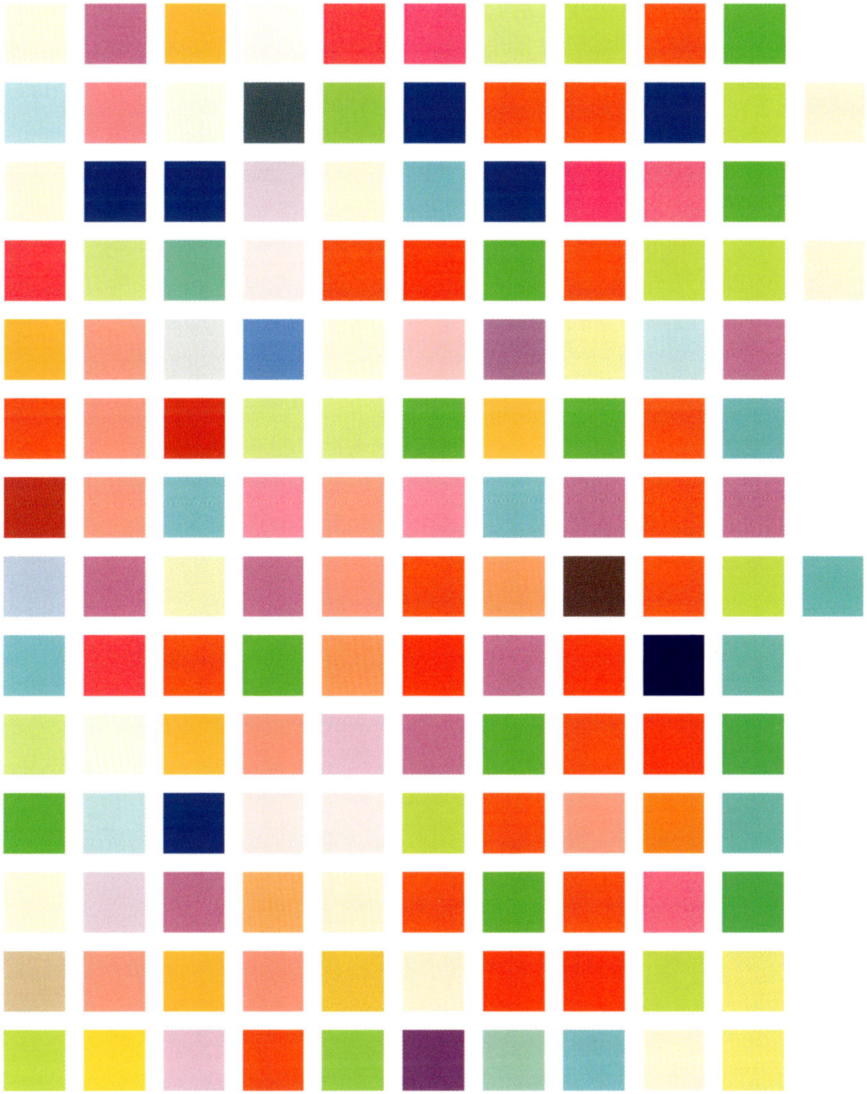

109.

110.

111.

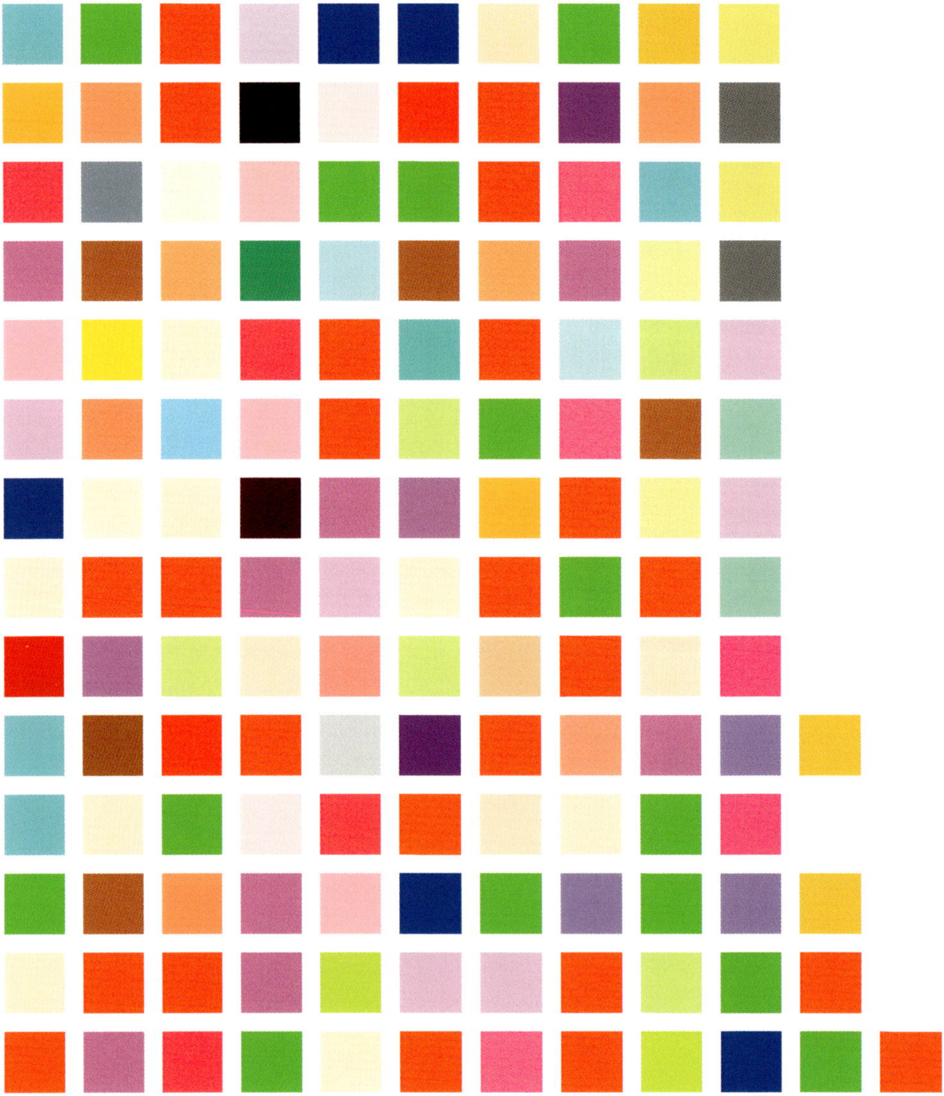

112.

113.

114.

115.

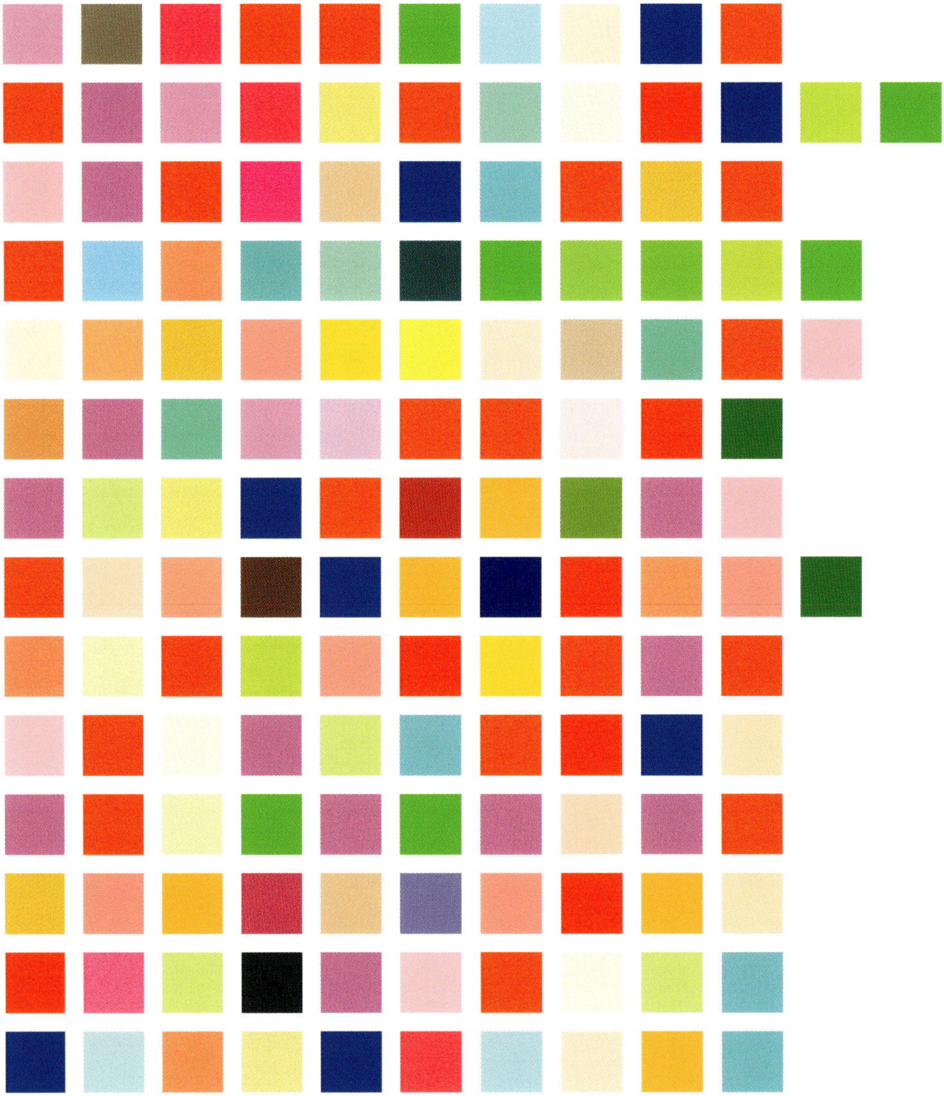

116.

117.

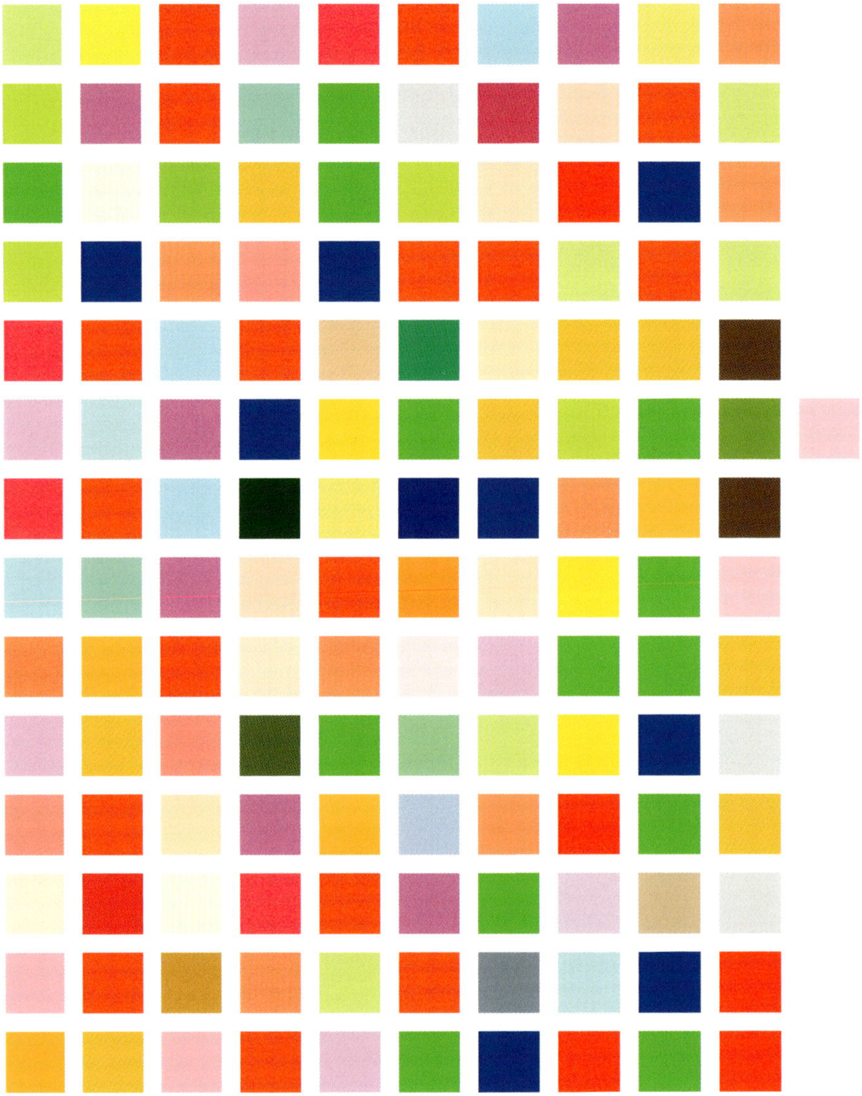

118.

119.

120.

121.

122.

123.

124.

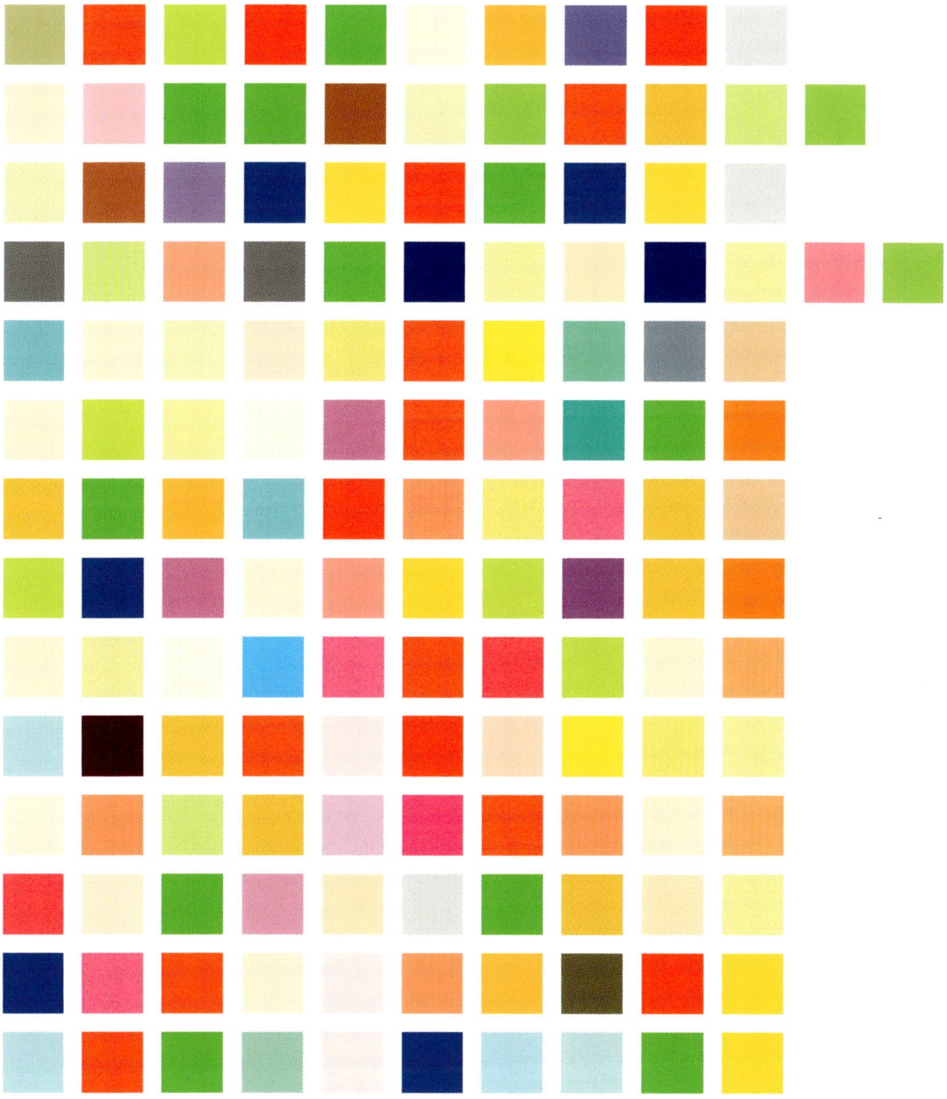

125.

126.

127.

128.

129.

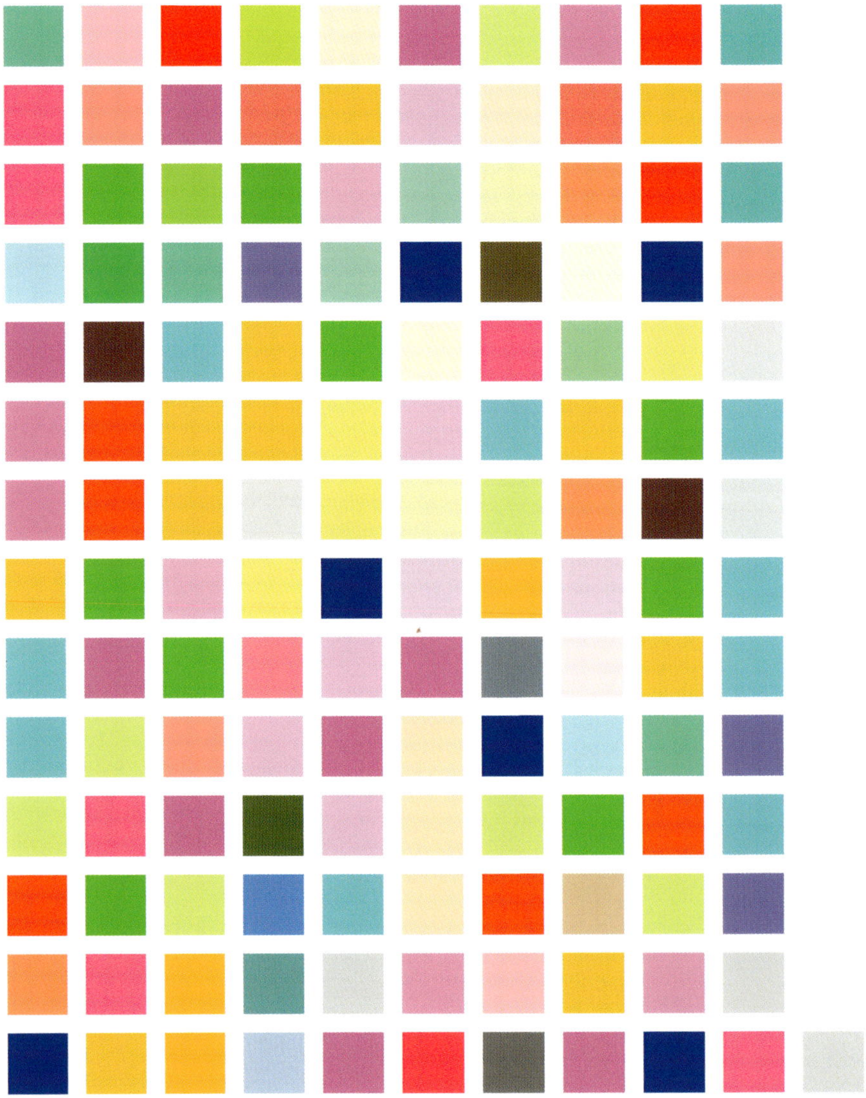

130.

131.

132.

133.

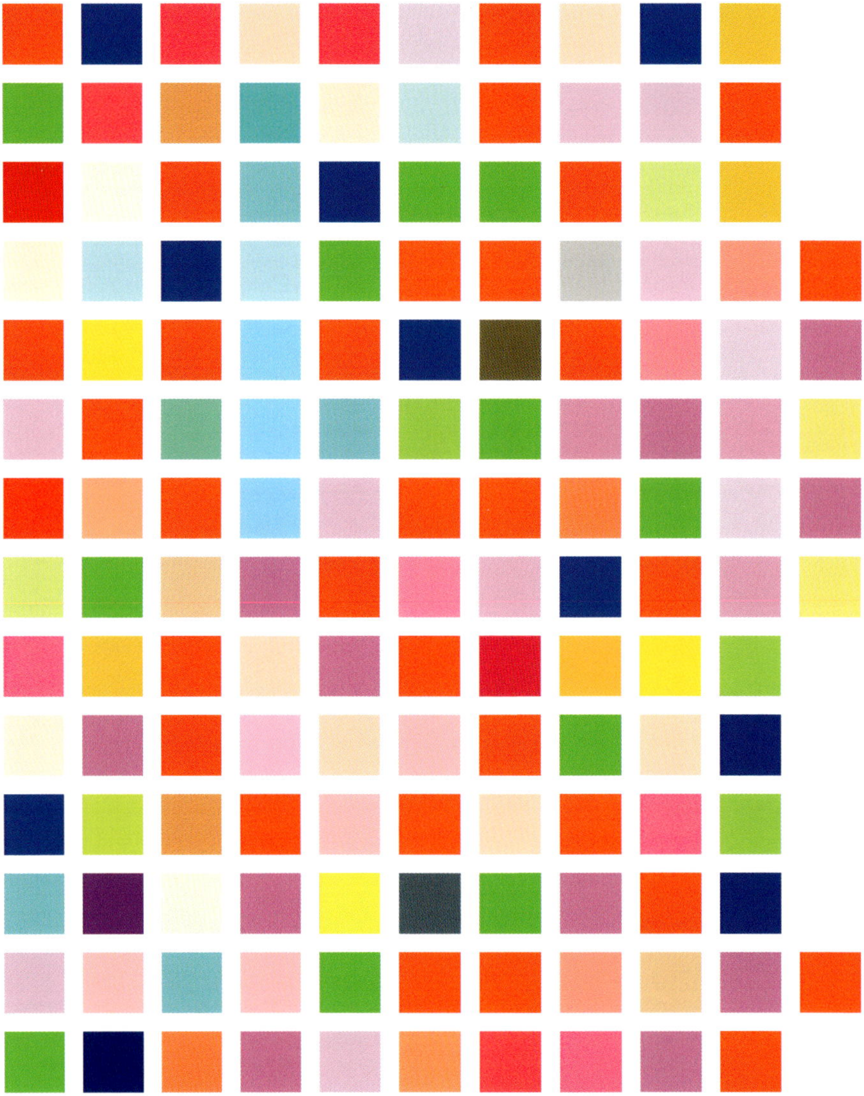

134.

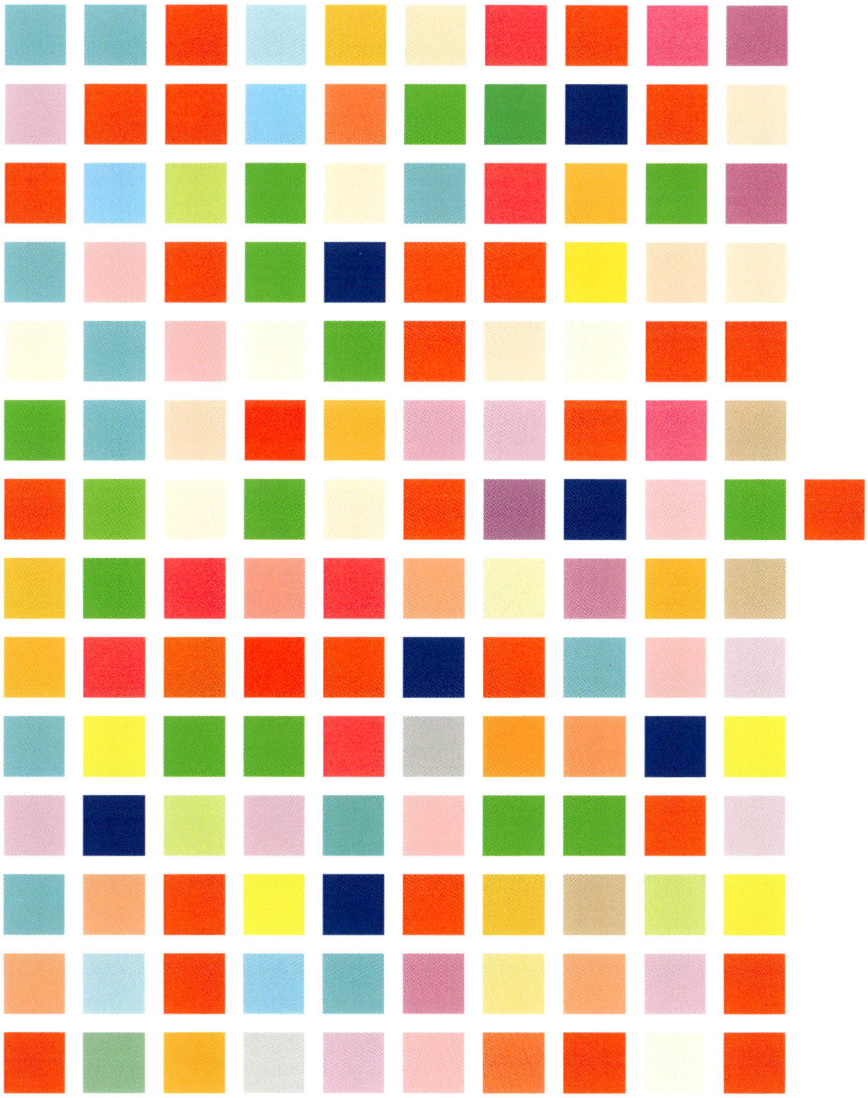

135.

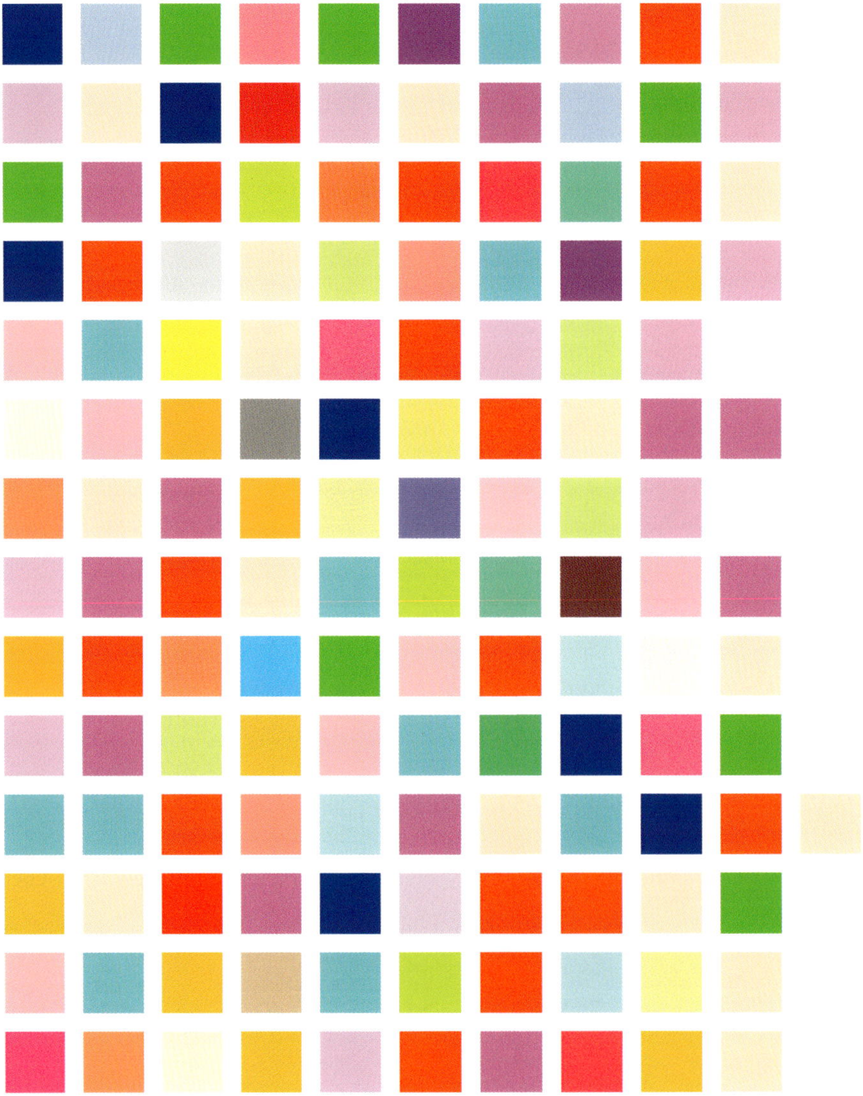

136.

137.

138.

139.

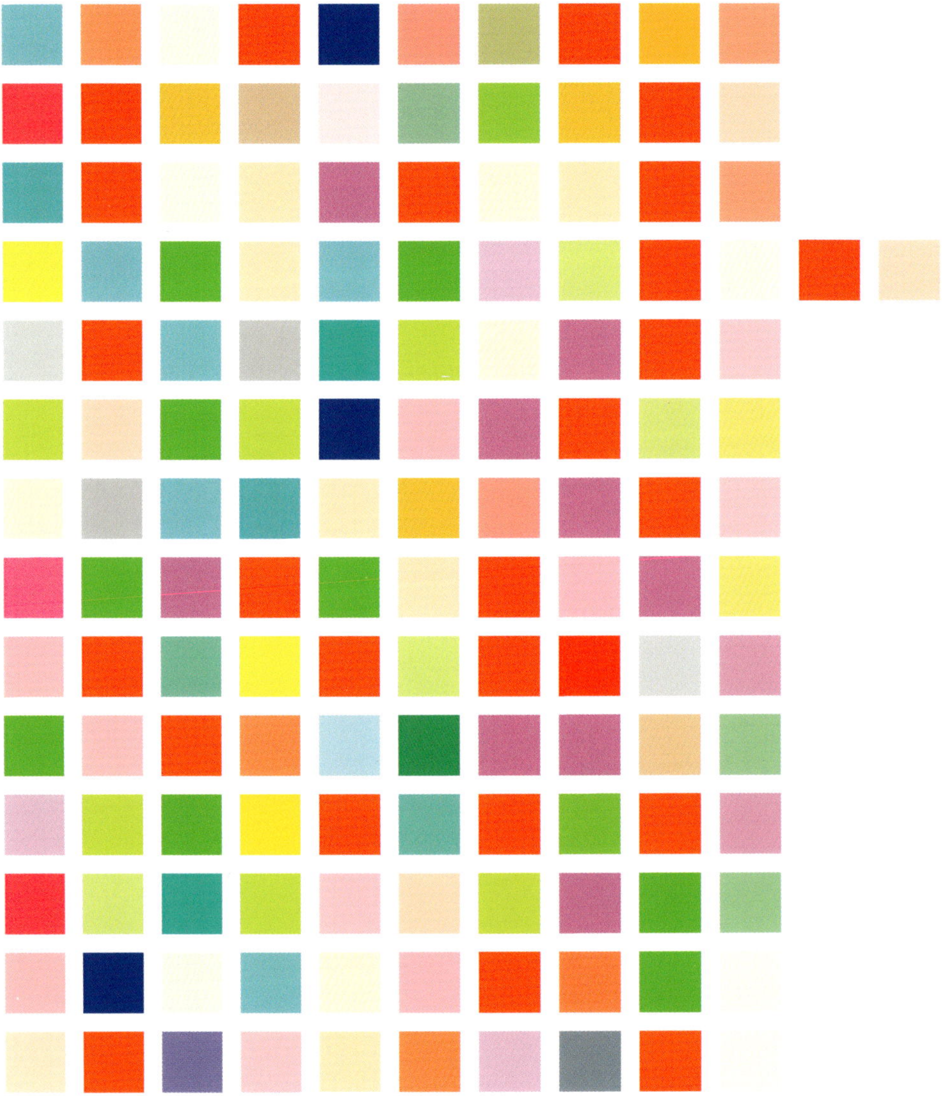

140.

141.

142.

143.

144.

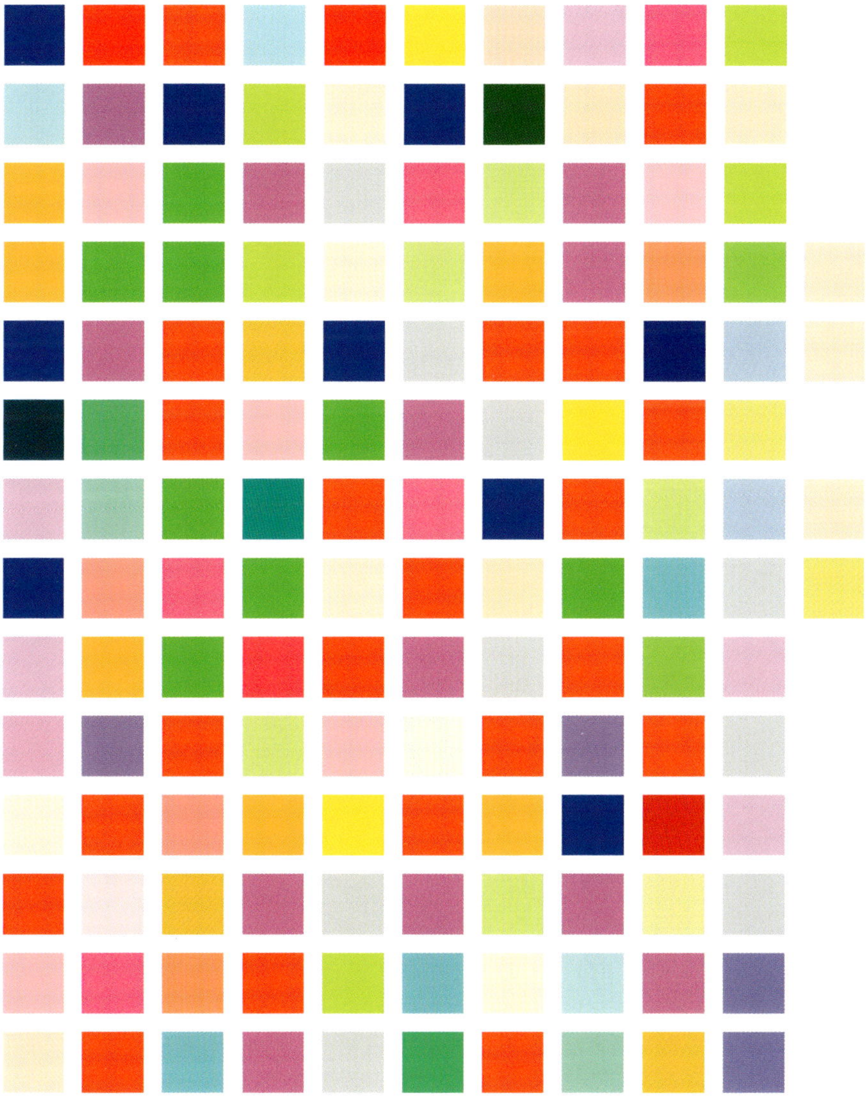

145.

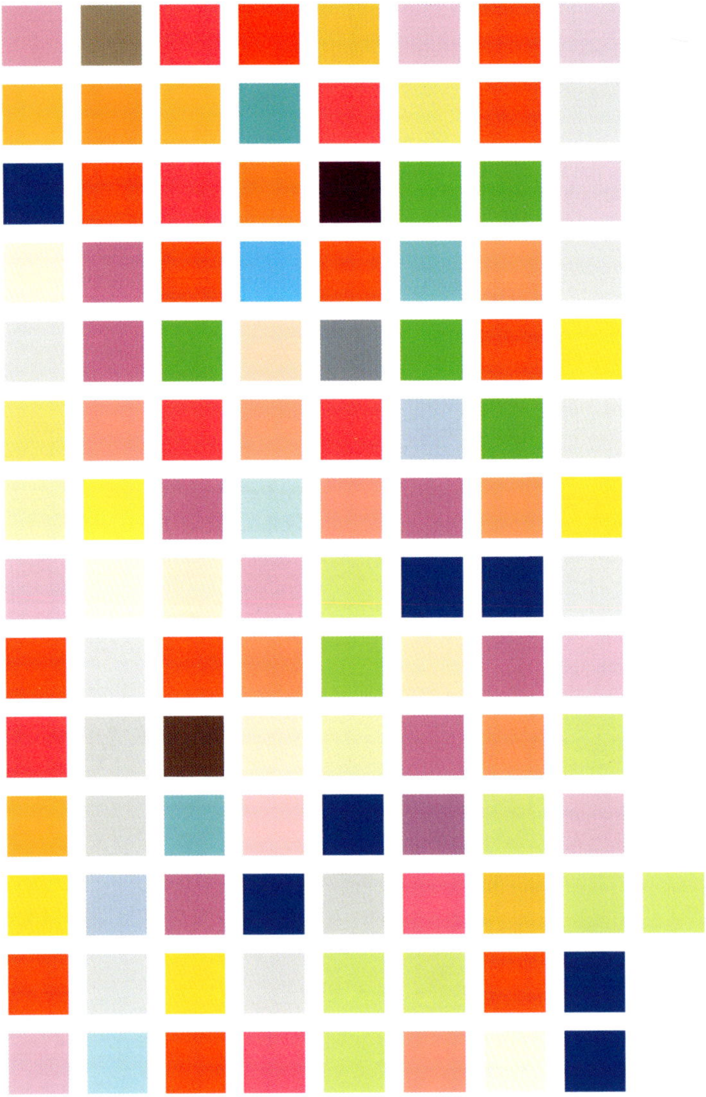

146.

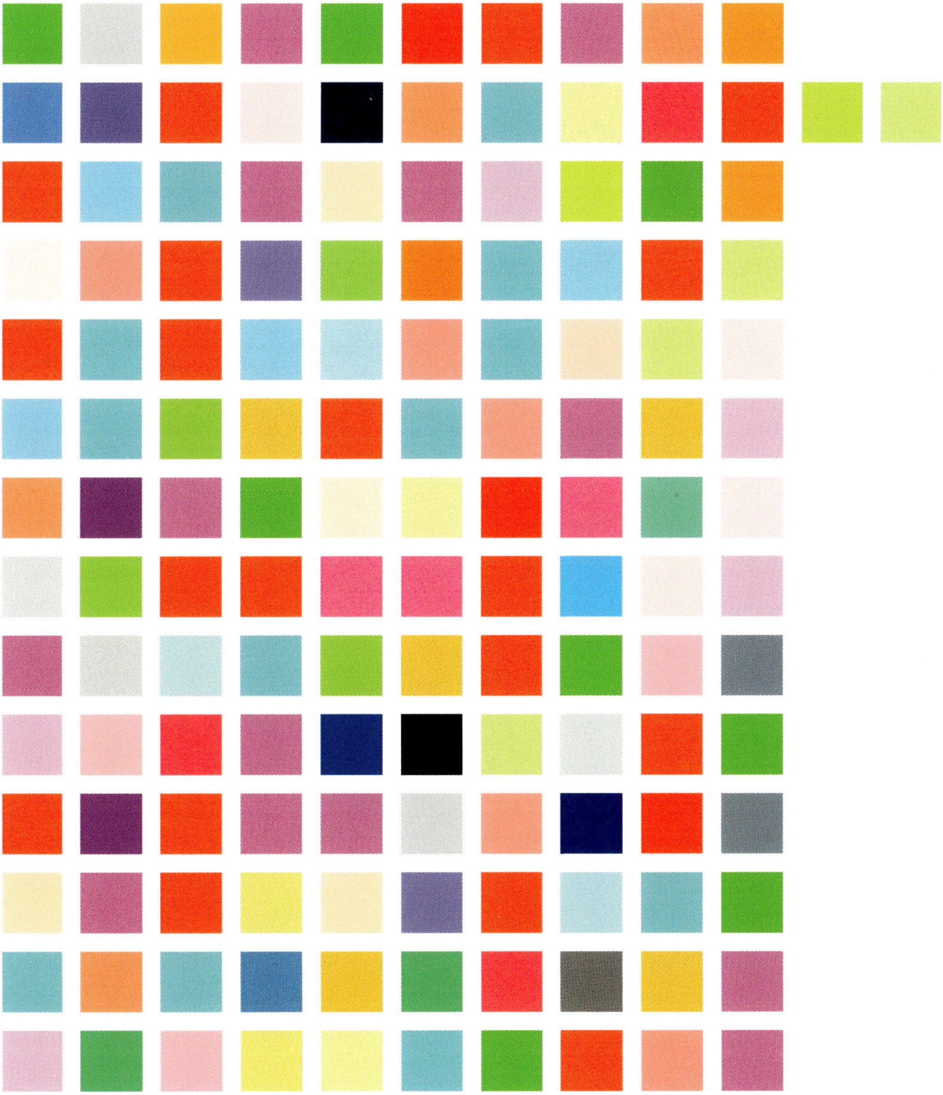

147.

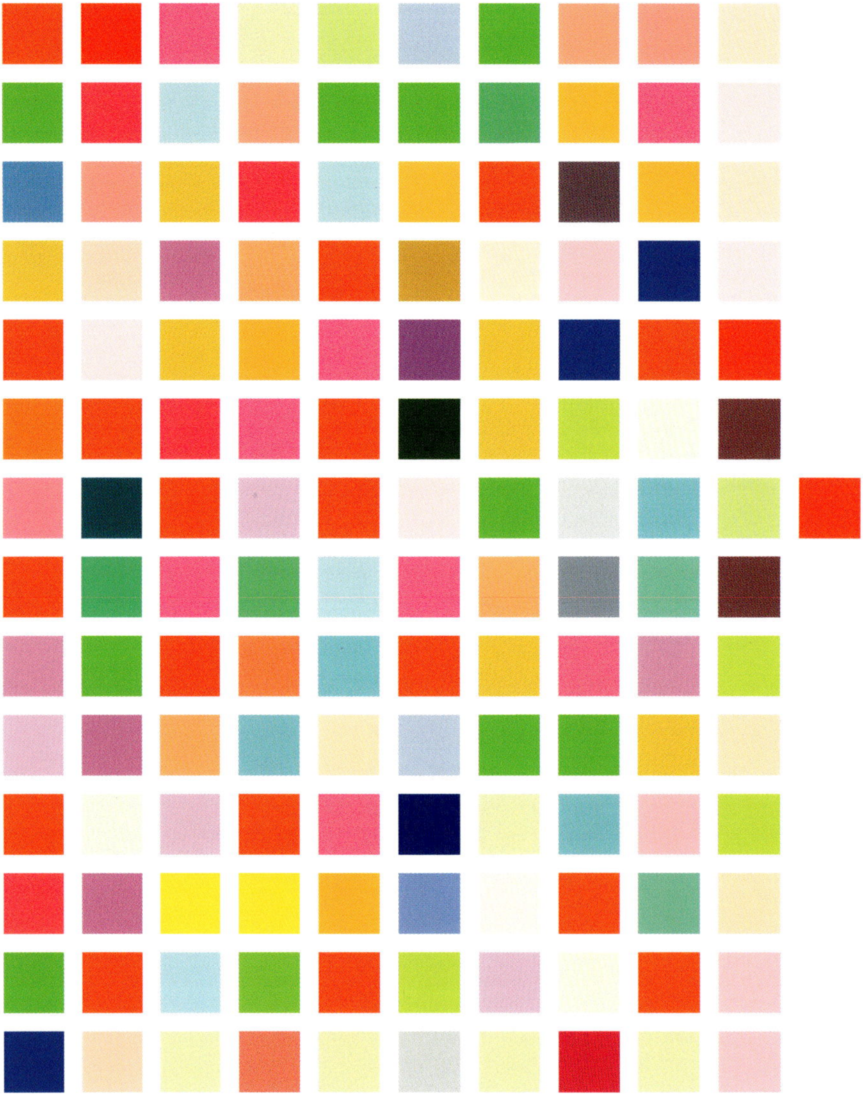

148.

149.

150.

151.

152.

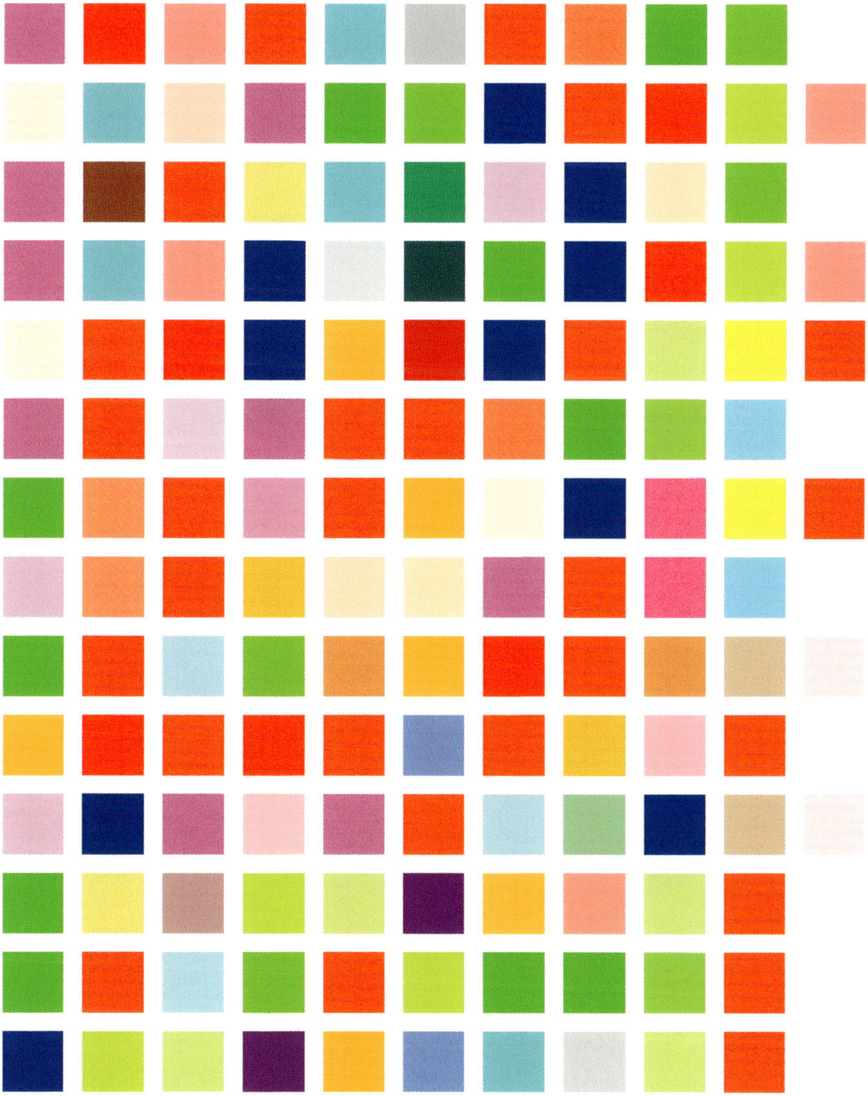

153.

154.

A Note on the Text

BardCode is an adaptation of William Shakespeare's *Sonnets* (1609) that turns the sounds of each word in the collection into a series of colour grids. Unlike conventional approaches to the sonnets, *BardCode* uses the syllable as the basic unit of interpretation for each word and line instead of the metre (the soft feet of iambs). Shakespeare bent, condensed, and stretched his words to fit the *stressed unstressed* rhythm of each line of iambic pentameter. Pronunciation in the original, thus, is informed by poetic convention. Shifting the focus away from the rhythm to the syllable alters the nature of the grid in these works. My copy text (if you will) was the 2002 *Oxford Shakespeare*, edited by Colin Burrow, and so all syllables follow the presentation there, where many elisions from the first quarto have been excised. I did not consult other editions but used this book unto itself as the basis for as many decisions about rhymes and syllables as possible. And indeed, there were many decisions that needed to be made for the sake of the art project. As an example, based on the metre, Shakespeare uses "cruel" as a one-syllable word in #131. However, just two sonnets earlier in #129, it is used as a two-syllable word—as it is again in #140 and #149, and so on. Similar issues arose with rhymes, which sometime stretched beyond contemporary ears and certainly his own. I have taken Shakespeare's sense of what rhymed, extrapolating from the end rhymes, as the basic rule of the project. Otherwise, as with the syllables, I have followed a maximalist tendency. The Sylchart that follows presents the sound of each syllable using the International Phonetic Alphabet (IPA) with their respective colour pairings, effectively the BardCode itself.

The Sylchart

208 different rhymes total across 154 sonnets
119 Shakespeare approved rhymes (determined by the 10th column)
20311 total syllables

ab (æb)	arve/erve (ɑ:v/ɜ:v)	**oat (əʊt)**	**ells/else (ɛlz/ɛls)**	ift (ɪft)	**oss/aws (ɒs/ɔ:z)**
abe (ayb)	ask (ɑ:sk)	ob (ɒb)	elp (ɛlp)	ig (ɪg)	**ot (ɔ:t)**
ace (eɪs)	ask'd (ɑ:skt)	ock/alk (lɒk/ɔ:k)	elth (ɛlθ)	**ight (aɪt)**	oud (aʊd)
ack (æk)	**ass/as (æs/æz)**	ode (əʊd)	elves/alves (ɛlvz/ ɑ:vZ)	ike (aɪk)	ound/own'd (u:nd/əʊnd)
act (ækt)	**ast/aste (ɑ:st/eɪst)**	ods (ɒdz)	em (ɛm)	ile (aɪl)	**ounds (aʊndz)**
ad (æd)	at (æt)	**of/oove (ɒv/u:v)**	emp/empt (ɛmp/ ɛmpt)	**ill (ɪl)**	**ount (aʊnt)**
ade/ied/ed (eɪd)	**atch/itch/etch (ætʃ/itʃ/ɛtʃ)**	**of'd/oov'd (ʌvd/u:vd)**	**ems (ɛmz)**	**ill'd (ɪld)**	ouse (aʊs)
afe (ayf)	ath (æθ)	off (ɒf)	**ence/ents/ants ɛns/ɛnts/ænts**	ilst/ist (aɪlst/ɪst)	**out (aʊt)**
aff (aaf)	**ave (eɪv/æv)**	oft/aft (ɒft/ɑ:ft)	encht (ɛntʃt)	**im/ims (ɪm/ɪmz)**	**owes (əʊz)**
ag (æg)	aw (ɔ)	og (ɒg)	**ends (ɛndz)**	**ime (aɪm)**	**owth (əʊθ)**
age (eɪdʒ)	ax/ex/ext/ixt (æks/ɛks/ɛkst/ɪkst)	**oh/ow/own (əʊ/aʊ/əʊn)**	engths (ɛŋθs)	**imm'd (ɪmd)**	**oy (ɔɪ)**
ail (eɪl)	**ay (eɪ)**	**oil'd (ɔɪld)**	**ent/ant (ɛnt/ænt)**	imp (ɪmp)	Qu (kw)
ain/an (eɪn/æn)	**aze (eɪz)**	oint/aint (ɔɪnt/eɪnt)	enth (ɛnθ)	inct (ɪŋkt)	**rg'd/g'd (ɔ:dʒd/gd)**
ained (eɪnd)	beb (ɛb)	òl'n (əʊlɒn)	ep (ɛp)	**ind/ind (aɪnd/ɪnd)**	the (ði:)
ains (eɪnz)	each (i:tʃ)	**old (əʊld)**	èpt/ipt (ɛpt/ɪpt)	**inds/inds (aɪndz/ɪndz)**	ub (ʌb)

ake/eek (eɪk/e:k)	eague (li:g)	on/un/own (ɒn/ʌn/əʊn)	erd/ord/ard (ɜ:d/ɔ:d/ɑ:d)	ine/in/en (aɪn/ɪn/ɛn)	uch (ʌʧ)
all/al (ɔ:l, æl)	eck/ic (ɛk/ɪk)	ond (ɒnd)	ere/ear/our/are (eə/ɪə/aʊə/ɑ:)	ines (aɪnz)	uck (ʌk)
alls/alse (ɔlz/ɔ́ls)	ect (ɛkt)	ongs (ɒŋz)	ers/orst (ɜ:st/ɔ:st)	ing (ɪŋ)	udst (ʊdst)
alt (ælt)	edge/udge/uge (ɛʤ/ʌʤ/u:ʤ)	ood/od (u:d/ɒd)	erse/hers/ours (ɜ:s/ɜ:z/aʊəz)	ings (ɪŋz)	uff (ʌf)
am (æm)	eds/eeds (ɛdz/i:dz)	oof (u:f)	esh (ɛʃ)	ink (ɪŋk)	ug (ʌg)
ame (eɪm)	eed (i:d)	ook (ʊk)	est/east (ɛst/i:st)	int (ɪnt)	uh (ə)
and, end (ænd, ɛnd)	eef (i:f)	ool (u:l)	et/ilt (ɛt/ɪlt)	ip (ɪp)	uk'd (ʌkt)
ang (æŋ)	eeks (i:ks)	oom/um (u:m/ʌm)	eth (ɛθ)	ipe (aɪp)	umph (ʌmf)
ange/arge (eɪnʤ/ɑ:ʤ)	eel (i:l)	oop (u:p)	ets (ɛts)	ips (ɪps)	ung/ong (ʌŋ/ɔŋ)
ank (æŋk)	eem (i:m)	oot (u:t)	ev (ɛv)	ire (aɪə)	unk (ʌŋk)
anst, ainst (ɑ:nst/ɛnst)	een (i:n)	ooth (u:θ)	eye/ee (aɪ/i:)	ish/ash/ush (ɪʃ/æʃ/ʌʃ)	uns (ʌnz)
ap (æp)	eep (i:p)	op (ɒp)	eyes (aɪz)	ish'd (ɪʃt)	up (ʌp)
ape (eɪp)	eese/ess (i:s/ɛs)	ope (əʊp)	ez (ɛz)	iss (ɪs)	ure/er/or (jʊə/ɜ:/ɔ:)
arch (ɑ:ʧ)	eet/ate (i:t/eɪt)	opt/upt (ɒpt/ʌpt)	ibes (aɪbz)	it (ɪt)	urge (:ʤ)
ark (ɑ:k)	ef (ɛf)	ork (ɔrk)	ice (aɪs)	ites (aɪts)	us (ʌs)
arn'd/orn'd (ɑ:nd/ɔ:nd)	eft (ɛft)	orlds/url (ɜ:ldz/ɜ:l)	id/ib (ɪd/ɪb)	ith (ɪð)	use (u:z)
arp (ɑ:p)	egg/ague (ɛg/eɪg)	orm/erm (ɔ:m/ɜ:m)	ides (aɪdz)	ive/ieve (ɪv/i:v)	ust (ʌst)
ars (ɑ:z)	eld (ɛld)	orn/ern (ɔ:n/ɜ:n)	ierce (ɪəs)	ix'd (ɪkst)	ut (ʌt)
arsh (ɑ:ʃ)	elf (ɛlf)	orse (ɔ:s)	if (ɪf)	oak (əʊk)	ute (ju:t)
art/ert (ɑ:t/ɜ:t)	elle/oll (ɛl/əʊl)	orth/earth (ɔ:θ/ɜ:θ)	ife (aɪf)	oast/ost (əʊst/ɒst)	you (ju:)
					z'd (ɛ)

Acknowledgements

The morning after the Text/Sound/Performance conference at University College Dublin, Gary Barwin, Christian Bök, and I set out on a cross-country excursion across Ireland. We drove in brilliant sunshine from Dublin to Limerick to Tralee to Portmagee and, finally, over to Valentia Island, talking of the conference, our lives, and everything in between ('feck ye', said all three to the barman). Valentia is a charmed space with easy access to both the first footprints on Earth, those tetrapods that were the first creatures to leave the sea for land, and the Skellig Michael Islands, the ancestral homeland of the Jedis. Future and past seemed intertwined there, as whisps of ocean spray hit both craggy rock and billboards promoting May the Fourth (be with you), when Star Wars fans descend upon the ancient village to travel in pilgrimage with the abundant dolphins to the Skellig Michaels. Communication and nature are similarly intertwined. It is the terminus for the first transatlantic telegraph cable that stretches over to Heart's Content, Newfoundland, and Glanleam House with its sub-tropical gardens and the mildest microclimate in Ireland. We drank whiskey before a peatmoss fire in our cabin in the foothills of Geokaun Mountain.

It was in that enchanted context that I first told my friends about a strange habit I had developed over the past nine months. During that time, I had commenced mapping out the relationships between all the syllables of all the poems across Shakespeare's *Sonnets*. Nothing could phase us there. They both saw the potential in the project immediately and offered insights and ideas for arrangement of the data I had collected. Christian teased me with the warning that I had five years to publish the project else it was up for grabs. As fate would have it, he wasn't the only one to try to claim the work, but as we walked to the local pub past lush sheepfields amidst relics of burnt-out famine homes, I could feel the book you are holding coming into being, propelled by friendship and the strange patterns of the world.

By the next summer, Gareth Jenkins had published the first sampling of the project with his press Apothecary Archive in Sydney, Australia. He released a beautiful, limited edition called *Sweet Forme*, followed by a second paperback edition when the first sold out. His support was enormous for moving the project forward. I would like to also thank Bill Ralph, Hallie Siegel, Derek Beaulieu, Linda Morra, Arnie McBay, Matthew Ellis, Neil Hennessy, Lori Emerson, Joakim Norling, Charles Bernstein, Amanda Earl, Jonathan Hope, M.J. Kidnie, Hai Hoang, Petra Schulze-Wollgast, Steve Remus, Natasha Pedros, Janet Mercer, Paul Dutton, and Paul Perry, whose support and enthusiasm propelled me to *just* meet Christian's deadline. I am extremely grateful to Anthony Etherin and Clara Daneri of Penteract Press for taking on the project and for realizing it so elegantly. You have been excellent company on this journey, indeed from those Dublin origins right through to publication. Lastly but not leastly, I tip my hat to the lovely Lisa, by whose side and for whose amusement I do all my scribblings. *Thy eternal summer shall not fade.*

Previous Titles

Monographs
Finding Nothing: The VanGardes, 1959-1975 (2021)
Avant-Garde Canadian Literature: The Early Manifestations (2013)

Poetry Books
The Fabulous Op (Co-written with Gary Barwin, 2022)
Foundry (2021)
Dazzle Pods (With Catherine Heard, 2021)
Sweet Forme: Shake-Speare's Perfect Sonnets (2020)
Boycott (2014)
This is Importance: A Students' Guide to Literature (2013)
The Obvious Flap (Co-written with Gary Barwin, 2011)
Psychic Geographies and Other Topics (2010)
The Others Raisd in Me (2009)
Haikube (With Matt Donovan and Hallie Siegal, 2006)
If Language (2005)

Editions
They Have Bodies: A Realistic Novel in Five Acts by Barney Allen (2020)
Avant Canada: Artists, Prophets, Revolutionaries
(Co-Edited with Christian Bök, 2019)
Space Between Her Lips:
The Selected Poetry of Margaret Christakos (2017)
Counterblasting Canada: Marshall McLuhan, Wyndham Lewis, Sheila Watson, and Wilfred Watson
(Co-Edited with Paul Hjartarson and Kristine Smitka, 2016)
RUSH: What Fuckan Theory; A Study uv Langwage by bill bissett
(Co-Edited with Derek Beaulieu, 2012)
The Wrong World: Bertram Brooker's Stories and Essays (2009)
Lawren Harris In the Ward: His Poetry and Painting (2007)
After Exile: A Raymond Knister Poetry Reader (2012)
W.W.E. Ross: Irrealities, Sonnets & Laconics
(Co-edited with Barry Callaghan, 2003)

Gregory Betts is a poet and professor at Brock University. His work consistently explores concrete, constrained, or collaborative poetics. He is the author of 11 books of poetry, including recent titles such as *Foundry* (Ireland 2021), *The Fabulous Op* (Ireland 2021, with Gary Barwin), and *Sweet Forme* (Australia 2020). His poems have been stenciled into the sidewalks of St. Catharines and selected by the SETI Institute to be implanted into the surface of the moon. He performed at the Vancouver 2010 Olympics, as part of the Cultural Olympiad, and has travelled and performed extensively across Canada, the US, and Europe. He is the curator of the bpNichol.ca Digital Archive, and author of the award-winning scholarly monographs *Finding Nothing: the VanGardes 1959-1975* and *Avant-Garde Canadian Literature.*